LOCHS
EXPLORING SCOTLAND'S FRESHWATER LOCHS

A FRANCES LINCOLN BOOK

Frances Lincoln Limited
4 Torriano Mews
Torriano Avenue
London NW5 2RZ
www.franceslincoln.com

Lochs: Exploring Scotland's Freshwater Lochs
Copyright © Julian Holland 2011
First Frances Lincoln edition 2011

All photographs by Julian Holland with the exception of pages:
93t; 118-9; 120-1; 126-7; 128b; 144-5 (all AA World Travel
Library) and 88-9 Brian Sharpe.

A catalogue record for this book is available from the British
Library.

ISBN 9780711231184

Printed and bound in China

1 2 3 4 5 6 7 8 9

Below *The sheltered bays on Loch Maree's southern shore are
overlooked by the mist shrouded peak of Slioch (3,218ft). The highest
peak on the north shore, the south ridge of this Munro is reached via an
eight-mile path from Kinlochewe to Letterewe.*

LOCHS
EXPLORING SCOTLAND'S FRESHWATER LOCHS

Julian Holland

F

FRANCES LINCOLN LIMITED
PUBLISHERS
www.franceslincoln.com

CONTENTS

Below *St Mary's Loch is the largest natural loch in the Borders Region of Scotland. Legend has it that the loch has no bottom and it is reputed to be the coldest in Scotland.*

Left *Set on a wooded hillside overlooking Loch Shin near Sallachy House is this beautiful grave of Count Ludwig Anton Von Saurma Hoym (1925-2004), a descendant of the House of Habsburg.*

Right *Nestling in the Black Cuillins on the Isle of Skye, Loch Coruisk's remoteness and wild, natural beauty have attracted writers, poets and artists for several centuries.*

Below *Wreathed in mist, the still and sheltered waters of Loch Ard are a popular location for canoeing and sailing while the surrounding vast tracts of Loch Ard Forest are a magnet for walkers and cyclists.*

Below inset *The steamship* Sir Walter Scott *has been carrying tourists across Loch Katrine for 110 years.*

INTRODUCTION

The hundreds of freshwater lochs that can be seen in Scotland today were shaped hundreds of thousands of years ago by the erosive power of the glacial ice sheets that once covered this northern part of Britain. During the 20th century some were turned into giant reservoirs by the building of dams, their waters harnessed for the generation of hydro-electricity. Despite these modern changes every loch has its own unique personality, their waters are famed for their fish while their shores are rich in flora and fauna - wild, remote and steeped in history, the many freshwater lochs of Scotland are among the most unspoilt and beautiful destinations to be found anywhere in Britain, if not the world.

Exploring Scotland's Freshwater Lochs gives an insight into the geology, historical background, myths and legends and natural history of over 30 Scottish freshwater lochs. Illustrated with specially commissioned colour photographs and supported by location maps, the text for each loch also includes details on walks, cycle rides, boat trips, angling, watersports, tourist information and accommodation.

EXPLORING SCOTLAND'S FRESHWATER LOCHS

THE RIGHT TO ROAM

The Land Reform (Scotland) Act 2003 allows universal access to land and inland water in Scotland. The act established the right to be on land for recreational, educational and certain other purposes and a right to cross land. However, the rights exist only if they are used responsibly and cannot interfere with activities including farming and game stalking. In Scotland these rights are greater than those granted in England and Wales. It must be pointed out that the rights in Scotland don't include vehicular access to private land and it also must be remembered that landowners' privacy must be respected.

SAFETY
Walking, cycling and climbing

Always be aware of possible changes in weather and check the forecast before you set out. Weather can change very quickly and at higher altitudes mist, fog rain and even snow can make route finding much more difficult. In this respect navigational skills are also essential. Away from the roads, novices should never tackle exploring Scotland's vast wildnerness areas without a suitably qualified local guide. Walkers and climbers should always be suitably equipped with warm inner clothing, waterproof outer clothing, rugged waterproof footwear, a map, compass, whistle, torch and emergency rations. Needless to say, offroad mountain bikers should be similarly equipped and also carry a basic set of tools and a puncture repair outfit.

Caneoing and kayaking

Scotland has some of the best accessible paddling environments in the world but lochs can be dangerous places - their deep, cold water and swiftly changing weather conditions can be fatal to the inexperienced. Safety gear must be carried and lifejackets worn at all times. If you are inexperienced never go out in a loch without a suitably qualified instructor and guide. The Scottish Canoe Association have details on access and the environment, coaching courses and safety. For more details contact the SCA, Caledonia House, South Gyle, Edinburgh EH12 9DQ (Tel. +44 (0) 131 3177314 or visit: www.canoescotland.org

Whether walking, climbing, cycling or paddling remember that mobile phones often do not receive a signal in these remote areas so it is essential that you inform someone of your planned trip before setting out.

ANGLING

Fishing in the majority of Scottish lochs is managed by local estates or local angling clubs. Each loch has different rules and regulations so anglers should always make themselves aware of these before setting out. Details on the purchase of permits and of boat hire can be found in this book's angling section of each loch.

WILD CAMPING & PROTECTING THE ENVIRONMENT

Wild camping is allowed on most unenclosed land in Scotland under the Land Reform (Scotland) Act 2003. With this right comes responsibilities and campers should leave these wild places undamaged by their visit. Sadly, in recent years there have been high profile cases of antiscocial behaviour at wild camping sites - for example the beautiful southeastern shore of Loch Lomond has been affected by drunken behaviour, vandalism, out of control fires, rubbish, abandoned equipment and unburied human waste. As usual, the minority ruin it for the majority and this case highlights how important it is to follow Scotland's Outdoor Access Code:

* Avoid overcrowding by moving on to a different location
* Carry a trowel to bury toilet waste and urinate well away from water courses
* Use a stove or leave no trace of any camp fire. Never cut down or damage trees
* Take away your rubbish and consider picking up other litter as well
* If in doubt ask the landowner
For more information visit:
www.outdooraccess-scotland.com

MIDGES

The female version of the Highland midge (*culicoides impunctatus*) is a fearsome insect as it can only lay eggs after it has had a meal of blood. Midges are found mainly in the north and west of Scotland, especially around lochs and rivers, between early June and the end of August. These insects are unavoidable so it always helps to have a suitable insect repellant to hand. You have been warned!

Above *In certain weather conditions Scottish lochs, such as Loch Arkaig, can look positively inviting but their extreme depth, cold water and swiftly changing weather conditions can prove fatal for the inexperienced paddler.*

WHERE TO FIND SCOTLAND'S FRESHWATER LOCHS

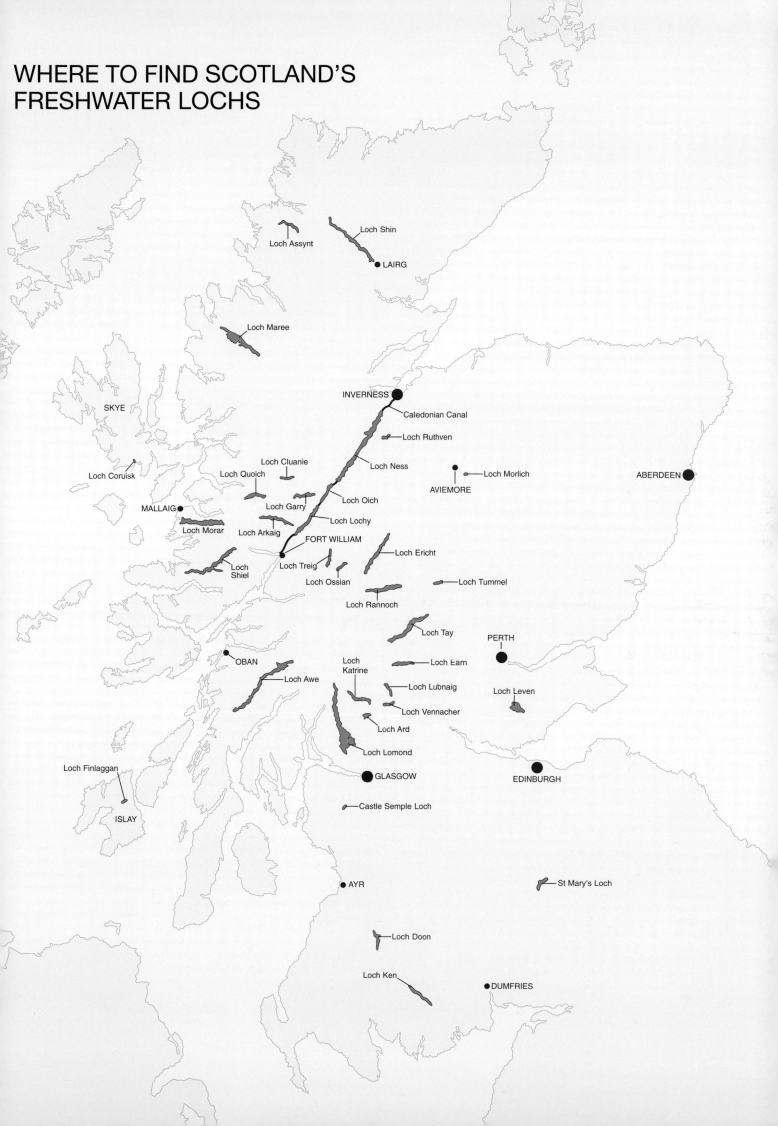

Loch Shin

Loch Assynt

LAIRG

Loch Maree

INVERNESS

SKYE

Caledonian Canal

Loch Ruthven

Loch Ness

Loch Coruisk

Loch Cluanie

Loch Quoich

Loch Morlich

ABERDEEN

AVIEMORE

Loch Garry

Loch Oich

MALLAIG

Loch Lochy

Loch Morar

Loch Arkaig

FORT WILLIAM

Loch Ericht

Loch Shiel

Loch Treig

Loch Ossian

Loch Tummel

Loch Rannoch

Loch Tay

PERTH

OBAN

Loch Earn

Loch Katrine

Loch Awe

Loch Lubnaig

Loch Leven

Loch Vennacher

Loch Ard

Loch Finlaggan

Loch Lomond

GLASGOW

EDINBURGH

ISLAY

Castle Semple Loch

AYR

St Mary's Loch

Loch Doon

Loch Ken

DUMFRIES

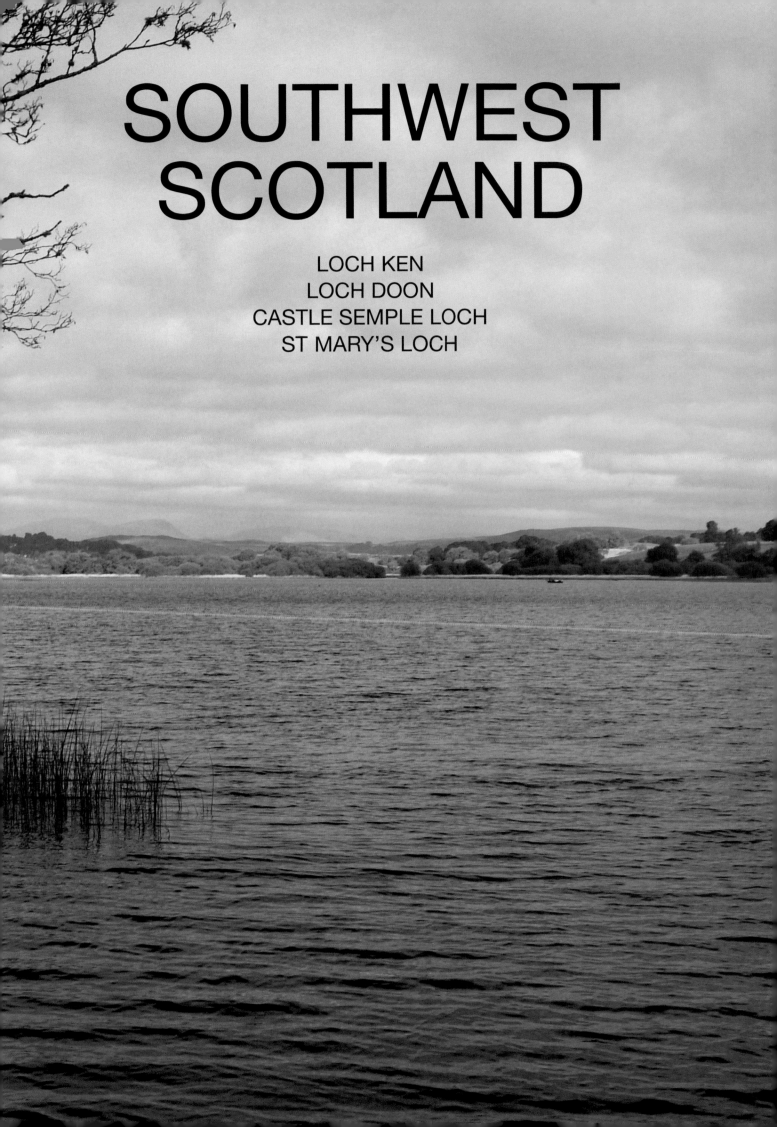

SOUTHWEST
SCOTLAND

LOCH KEN
LOCH DOON
CASTLE SEMPLE LOCH
ST MARY'S LOCH

LOCH KEN VITAL STATISTICS
Max. length: 8.7mi
Surface area: 4.32mi²
Average depth: 49ft
Max. depth: 82ft
Water volume: 36 billion gallons

ORDNANCE SURVEY 1: 50,000
LANDRANGER MAPS
No. 77/83

LOCH KEN

Below *Loch Ken has a good reputation among anglers for its pike, roach and perch. Salmon run through during the season while other species to be caught include brown trout, ruffe, bream, dace and rainbow trout.*

Transformed from a river into a large freshwater reservoir during the construction of the Galloway hydro-electric scheme in the 1930s, Loch Ken is a long and narrow finger of water set in an area of great natural beauty. Its popularity as a watersports venue appears to sit comfortably with its importance as an environmentally sensitive area. The loch is fed by the Water of Ken from the north and by the River Dee from the west. At the southern end the Glenlochar Barrage controls outflow along the River Dee to the Tongland power station.

HISTORY
The Pictish tribes that once inhabited Scotland were a thorn in the side for the Roman occupiers of Britain. The Novantae tribe of Galloway were no exception and several military campaigns were mounted against them by the Roman governor, Gnaeus Julius Agricola, around 81AD. Covering seven acres, the remains of a Roman fort used as a springboard for these campaigns can be seen today on the east bank of the River Dee near the Glenlochar Barrage.

Many turbulent centuries followed the

Roman withdrawal with early Christians being ousted from their abbey at Glenlochar following invasion by the Danes in the 10th century. During the 12th and 13th centuries the Lords of Galloway who ruled this region came under threat from Anglo-Norman settlers who were given grants of land in return for providing military service. A Norman motte, or defensive mound, from this period can be seen on the north shore of Loch Ken at Parton.

At the northern end of the loch are the ruins of Kenmure Castle, set on a rocky knoll that is said to have been occupied by the Lords of Galloway from the 12th century. The present castle was built in the early 16th century and was

Above *This rusting bowstring bridge north of Parton once carried the Dumfries to Stranraer railway line across Loch Ken. The railway opened in 1861 and, in 1965, became one of the first railways to close in Scotland following publication of the 'Beeching Report'.*

the principal residence of the Gordons of Lochinvar. The castle had a turbulent history – it was besieged and destroyed in 1568 following which it was rebuilt only to be damaged again by Cromwell's troops in 1650. Following extensive modifications in the 19th century the castle ended its days as a hotel after World War II before being made roofless and gutted by a fire in the early 1950s.

Railways came to this part of Galloway in 1861 when the Portpatrick Railway opened between Castle Douglas and Stranraer. Sadly, this scenic line became an early victim of Dr Beeching's 'Axe' and it closed in 1965. The rusting bowstring bridge that once carried the railway over Loch Ken near Parton still stands today although its structure is considered unsafe to cross.

The construction of the Galloway Hydro-Electric Scheme in the 1930s totally transformed the valley of the River Dee and, on its completion in 1936, had created the loch that we know today. The scheme includes seven reservoirs, nine dams or barrages, six tunnels and aqueducts and six power stations. Glenlochar Barrage, at the southern end of the loch, is operated by remote control to regulate the flow of water down the River Dee to the Tongland power station north of Kirkcudbright.

NATURAL HISTORY

Set in an area of great natural beauty, Loch Ken is designated a Regional Scenic Area and is part of an Environmentally Sensitive Area. Parts of the loch including Kenmure Holms at the northern end are designated as Sites of Special Scientific Interest and as Special Protection Areas for their importance as overwintering sites for Greenland white-fronted and Icelandic greylag geese.

The Galloway Red Kite Trail around Loch Ken includes four hides and a feeding station that provide opportunities to view these spectacular birds. For more information visit: www.gallowaykitetrail.com

An RSPB Reserve on the Hensol Estate midway up the loch on its western shore comprises a mixture of ancient broadleaved woodland and freshwater marsh. Several hides in the reserve can be reached on foot from the car park at Mains of Duchrae. The reserve contains many species of interest including great spotted woodpecker, willow tit, barn owl, nuthatch, red kite and red squirrel. In the summer numerous woodland birds include pied flycatcher and redstart. During the winter months the surrounding fields support up to 300 Greenland white-fronted geese.

WALKING AND CYCLING

The reasonably level Galloway Red Kite Trail around Loch Ken is ideal for cyclists. The 24-mile Trail is extended by 14 miles of forest trails in the summer months. (see NATURAL HISTORY).

While the shoreline of Loch Ken is virtually ringed by roads, the vast Galloway Forest Park to the west, at the northern end of the loch, offers unlimited opportunities for walkers and mountain bikers. A Forestry Commission car park at Bennan on the A762 gives access to a viewpoint, waymarked trails, a circular walk and an old cattle drovers road, the Raiders Road Forest Drive, to Clatteringshaw Loch. Both Route 7 of the National Cycle Network and the Southern Upland Way long distance path pass alongside the latter loch near Raploch Moor where Robert the Bruce defeated the English in 1307.

For more information about the Park visit: www.forestrycommission.gov.uk/gallowayforestpark

WATER SPORTS

Loch Ken is a popular venue for water sports including wind surfing, sailing, rowing, canoeing and water skiing. For details of activities, parking, launching and mooring fees contact:
Loch Ken Holiday Park, Parton, Castle Douglas, Dumfries & Galloway DG7 3NE
Tel. +44 (0) 1644 470282
Website: www.lochkenholidaypark.co.uk
    or
Galloway Activity Centre, Parton, Castle Douglas DG7 3NQ
Tel. +44 (0) 1644 420626
Website: www.lochken.co.uk

ANGLING AND BOAT HIRE

Loch Ken has a good reputation among anglers for its pike, roach and perch. Salmon run through during the season while other species to be caught include brown trout, ruffe, bream, dace and rainbow trout. The main fishing areas are conveniently next to the A762 on the west shore and next to the A713 immediately north of the railway bridge on the east shore. Permits, rowing and motor boat hire can be arranged through Loch Ken Holiday Park (see WATER SPORTS).

TOURIST INFORMATION AND ACCOMMODATION

Castle Douglas Tourist Information Centre, Markethill Car Park, Castle Douglas, Dumfries & Galloway DG7 1AE
Tel. +44 (0) 1556 502611
Website: www.visitscotland.com

Below *By 1936 rising water levels caused by the construction of the Galloway Hydro-Electric Scheme had created the Loch Ken that we know today. Glenlochar Barrage, at the southern end of the loch, regulates the flow of water down the River Dee to the Tongland power station to the north of Kirkcudbright.*

LOCH DOON

LOCH DOON
VITAL STATISTICS
Max. length: 5.6mi
Surface area: 2.78mi²
Average depth: 20ft
Max. depth: 108ft
Water volume: 9.6
billion gallons

ORDNANCE
SURVEY 1: 50,000
LANDRANGER MAP
NO. 77

The largest natural freshwater loch in southern Scotland, Loch Doon is surrounded to the west and south by the afforested mountain slopes of the Galloway Forest Park. To the north lie the coal and iron deposits that were once mined around the village of Dalmellington.

A reservoir for hydro-electricity generation since the 1930s, the loch is fed by the waters from several smaller lochs to the south and west. Loch Doon outflows at its northern end via the dramatic Ness Glen and the River Doon - the latter immortalised by Robert Burns in his famous poem *Ye banks and braes O' bonnie Doon*.

HISTORY

Loch Doon Castle stands today on the west shore of the loch near the settlement of Craigmalloch. However this wasn't alway the case as the eleven-sided curtain-walled castle was originally built by the Earl of Carrick on an island in the loch in the 13th century. In fact the island was probably occupied much earlier than this as several ancient wooden canoes and weapons were excavated here in the 19th century.

The castle, designed by Sir Christopher Seton, the brother-in-law of Robert the Bruce, changed hands several

Below *The building of a dam in the 1930s led to the level of water in Loch Doon rising by 30ft. Several secrets now lie beneath the surface including World War I seaplane hangers and Castle Island. A World War II Spitfire was brought to the surface in 1982.*

Right *Saved from a watery grave in the 1930s, Loch Doon Castle was dismantled and then rebuilt on its present sight after rising water levels threatened its island home.*

times. It was first seized by the English after the Battle of Methven during the Wars of Scottish Independence in 1306 but later retaken by the Kennedy family and held by them until 1511 when it was taken by William Crauford of Lefnoris. The castle finally met its end a few years later when it was destroyed during the reign of James V. For over 400 years the ruins of Loch Doon Castle remained untouched until the 1930s when the loch's water levels were raised during the building of a dam for the Galloway hydro-electric scheme. As the water levels rose the outer walls of the castle were

dismantled and rebuilt stone by stone on the western shore. The remains of Castle Island can still be seen in the loch during prolonged periods of drought.

Loch Doon Castle was not the only man-made structure to suffer when water levels rose 30ft in 1936. Seaplane hangers, built during World War I on the west shore of the loch as part of an ill-fated gunnery school located near Dalmellington, were also submerged.

Secrets of World War II were discovered in the loch when a Spitfire aircraft of the 312 (Czech) Squadron that had crashed here in 1941 was raised to the surface in 1982. The aircraft is currently being restored at the Dumfries Aviation Museum. For more details visit: www.dumfriesaviationmuseum.com

NATURAL HISTORY

Surrounded by spectacular scenery, Loch Doon has been designated as a Site of

Below *Loch Doon is surrounded by magnificent scenery and enormous tracts of commercial coniferous forests. To the south is the Galloway Forest Park - 300 square miles of remote wilderness managed by the Forestry Commission since 1947.*

Special Scientific Interest because of the rare Arctic char that inhabit its waters. Regular visitors to the loch include golden eye, merganser and sandpiper.

Much of Loch Doon is also set in the northern part of the vast Galloway Forest Park. Established by the Forestry Commission in 1947, it is Britain's largest forest park and covers an area of 300 square miles. With numerous small lochs, moorland, vast tracts of Sitka Spruce forests and craggy mountain peaks (Merrick is the highest at 2,765ft), the forest park is home to a wide variety of birds and mammals including goldcrest, nightjar, golden eagle, black grouse, red kite, osprey, red squirrel, red, roe and fallow deer, pine marten and otter. With some of the least polluted night skies in Europe, the Park is also a favourite destination for star gazers.

For more information about the Park visit: www.forestrycommission.gov.uk/gallowayforestpark

At the northern end of the loch, the impressive rocky gorge of Ness Glen is also a Site of Special Scientic Interest for its rare mosses and ferns.

WALKING AND CYCLING

There are miles of forest trails suitable for walkers or mountain bikers in the Galloway Forest Park. Away from these trails the Park is a remote wilderness and a paradise for experienced hillwalkers. Access to the Park from Loch Doon is from the Forestry Commission car park on the west shore, south of Craigmalloch. A whole day should be set aside for the circular walk around the loch.

CANOEING AND KAYAKING

Loch Doon can be accessed from the few marked car parks along the west shore although many access points to the loch have recently been blocked off by large boulders. Ness Glen, at the northern end of the loch, provides challenging white water only suitable for experienced kayakers. Note that overnight parking alongside the loch is forbidden and is enforced by the Forestry Commission's rangers.

ANGLING

Fishing by rod and line for wild brown trout, Arctic char and perch does not require a permit. Day permits for salmon fishing on the River Doon at the north end of the loch are available from Craigengillan Estate (Tel. +44 (0) 1292 551818 or visit www.craigengillan.com.

TOURIST INFORMATION AND ACCOMMODATION

Ayr Tourist Information Centre, 22 Sandgate, Ayr, Ayrshire KA7 1BW
Tel. +44 (0) 1292 290300
Website: www.visitscotland.com

Right *Designated a Site of Special Scientific Interest for its population of rare Arctic char, Loch Doon is popular with anglers on bank or boat. Its clear waters also support wild brown trout and perch.*

CASTLE SEMPLE LOCH

Easily accessed by public transport and located only 12 miles southwest of Glasgow, Castle Semple Loch is not only a popular watersports centre but also an important nature reserve. Once part of an 18th century estate, the loch now falls within the Clyde Muirshiel Regional Park.

HISTORY

Castle Semple Loch is named after a large mansion house that was built in 1735 on the site of 16th century Castle Tower. The latter building was a replacement for Elliston Castle at Howwood to the northeast of the loch. Set in a 900-acre estate, Castle Semple was built in an elaborate gothic style for Col William MacDowell. It was destroyed in a fire in 1924 and demolished in 1960.

Set on the banks of the River Calder at the southwest end of the loch, the village of Lochwinnoch was once an important centre for grain and cotton mills and the bleaching and furniture industries in the 17th and 18th centuries.

There were once railways running down each side of the loch. On the east bank the Glasgow to Ayr main line opened in 1840 and is still open for business today. To cope with increased traffic on that line a parallel line was opened along the west bank of the loch in 1905. It closed to passengers in 1966.

NATURAL HISTORY

Castle Semple Loch and Barr Loch to the south are both designated as Sites of Special Scientific Interest for their important wetland habitats. As part of the Clyde Muirshiel Regional Park, Lochwinnoch RSPB Nature Reserve and Castle Semple Country Park are important overwintering wildfowl sanctuaries with around 160 species of birds, including great crested grebe, goosander, red-breasted merganser and water rail, being recorded. An RSPB Visitor Centre is located at the south end of the loch.

Lochside Parkhill Wood is home to blackcap, garden warbler, chiffchaff, whitethroat and sedge warbler during the spring and summer months. For more information on woodland walks and nature trails contact the Castle Semple Visitor Centre, Lochlip Road, Lochwinnoch, Renfrewshire PA12 4EA (Tel. +44 (0) 1505 842882 or visit: www.clydemuirshiel.co.uk)

WALKING AND CYCLING

Now a footpath and cycleway (part of National Cycle Network Route 7), the former railway line from Johnstone to Kilburnie passes along the western shore of the loch. Mountain bikes can be hired from Castle Semple Visitor Centre.

CASTLE SEMPLE LOCH
VITAL STATISTICS
Max. length: 1.42mi
Surface area: 0.26mi²
Average depth: 10ft
Max. depth: 39ft
Water volume: 450 million gallons
ORDNANCE SURVEY 1: 50,000 LANDRANGER MAP NO. 63

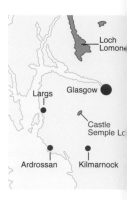

Right *Watersports and wildlife rub shoulders comfortably on Castle Semple Loch. As one of the few wetlands left in western Scotland, the RSPB reserve at Lochwinnoch is home to a wide variety of waterfowl during the winter months. In the spring the elaborate displays of the great crested grebe attract much attention. For more information visit: www.rspb.org.uk*

CANOEING, KAYAKING AND SAILING

Castle Semple Loch is renowned for its watersports facilities. Recognised by the Royal Yachting Association, the Visitor Centre offers courses in sailing, canoeing and kayaking. Hire facilities are available.

ANGLING AND BOAT HIRE

Excellent coarse fishing for pike, roach, perch and eel. Salmon and sea trout pass through on their journey to the River Calder. Angling on the loch is managed by the St Winnoch Angling Club. For more information and permit outlets visit: www.lochwinnochac.net

TOURIST INFORMATION AND ACCOMMODATION

Largs Tourist Information Centre, The Railway Station, Main Street, Largs, Ayrshire KA30 8AN
Tel. +44 (0) 1475 689962
Website: www.visitscotland.com

Left *By the end of the 19th century the Glasgow to Ayr main line's capacity had become stretched to the limit. Widening it along the east shore of Castle Semple Loch was not possible so the Glasgow & South Western Railway opened a parallel line from Johnstone along the west shore of the loch. Closure came in 1966 and since then it has been transformed into a well-surfaced footpath and cycleway. It now forms part of National Cycle Network Route 7.*

ST MARY'S LOCH

St Mary's Loch
Vital Statistics
Max. length: 2.79mi
Surface area: 1.39mi²
Average depth: 65.6ft
Max. depth: 131ft
Water volume: 15.8
billion gallons

Ordnance
Survey 1: 50,000
Landranger Map
No. 73

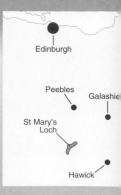

The largest natural freshwater loch in the Scottish Borders, St Mary's Loch was created by glacial action during the last Ice Age. Around 10,000 years ago it was a much larger loch but debris carried down by mountain streams split it into two and formed the narrow isthmus that now separates it from the Loch of the Clewes. The loch outflows along the River Yarrow to the River Tweed. St Mary's loch has two claims to fame: its waters are supposedly the coldest in Scotland and, apparently, it has no bottom!

HISTORY

Once covered by native woodland the valleys of the Ettrick and Yarrow were a refuge for William Wallace and his followers during the Wars of Independence in the late 13th century. Dating from the troubled times of the 14th-16th centuries, defensive towers, such as the one found at Dryhope to the north of the loch, are a common feature in the Borders. Religious oppression has also left its mark on the area – still practised on the last Sunday in July in the churchyard of St Mary's Kirk of the Lowes, 'Blanket Preaching' is believed to have taken place here since the 17th century when covenanting preachers were fighting to establish Presbyterianism in Scotland. Suffering from religious oppression by Charles I, preachers were banned from holding a church service so they and their flock gathered together on the hillside, sheltering under blankets.

At the southern end of the loch, Tibbie Shiels Inn has strong connections with Scottish literary figures. The inn was founded by Tibbie Shiel who was, in her early years, a servant of the parents of the famous Scottish writer, James Hogg. Born in nearby Ettrick around 1770, James Hogg went on to become a famous satirical writer and poet during the early 19th century. He counted among his friends Sir Walter Scott and William Wordsworth, the latter writing a eulogy when Hogg died in 1835.

In the meantime Tibbie Shiel went on to marry a molecatcher and have six children. They all lived in a cottage at the southern end of St Mary's Loch and it was here, following her husband's death in 1824, that Tibbie became an

innkeeper. The inn was a popular haunt for writers and poets until Tibbie's death in 1878 at the age of 95. Still to be seen today, a statue to James Hogg was erected on the hillside overlooking the inn and the loch in 1860.

NATURAL HISTORY

The native deciduous woodlands that once grew on the lower hills around St Mary's Loch have virtually all disappeared. In places they have been replaced by commercial coniferous species such as the Sitka spruce that can be seen on the eastern shore of the loch. While the upland areas are used for sheep grazing and heather moorland managed for red grouse shooting, the poorer grassland and bogs support much plant life including heath bedstraw, tormentil, butterwort, marsh thistle and the heath spotted orchid. Birdlife on the surrounding hills includes the meadow pipit, buzzard, short-eared owl and black grouse. In the loch are mallard, pochard, goosander and overwintering goldeneye and whooper swan. The Arctic char that once lived in the loch have unfortunately all been fished out.

WALKING

Nestling in the Southern Uplands, St Mary's Loch is a little-known gem, virtually unspoilt by human activity. This is hillwalking country at its best and the Southern Upland Way long distance path follow the loch's eastern shore on its 212-mile route between Portpatrick and Cockburnspath. The car park near Tibbie Shiels Inn is an ideal starting point for hillwalking or the six-mile return walk alongside the loch.

CANOEING, KAYAKING AND SAILING

Anyone can make use of the loch in an unpowered boat but access is not allowed from the St Mary's Loch Sailing Club at its southern end.

A word of caution: St Mary's Loch is very deep, cold and can often be very windy. For information on membership of the sailing club visit: www.stmlsc.org.uk

ANGLING AND BOAT HIRE

The St Mary's Loch Angling Club leases the trout and coarse fishing rights for the loch and neighbouring Loch of the Lowes. For more information on the club visit: stmarysloch.googlepages.com

Fishing for brown trout, pike, perch and eel is by boat or bank. Permits and boat hire are available from the Loch Keeper's Cottage in Cappercleuch (Tel. +44 (0) 1750 42329). Permits are also available from the Tibbie Shiels Inn (see below).

TOURIST INFORMATION AND ACCOMMODATION

Tibbie Shiels Inn, St Mary's Loch, Selkirkshire TD7 5LH
Tel. +44 (0) 1750 42231
Website: www.tibbieshiels.com

Moffat Tourist Information Centre, Churchgate, Moffat, Dumfries & Galloway DG10 9EG Tel. +44 (0) 1683 220620 Website: www.visitdumfriesandgalloway.co.uk

Below *Nestling in the Southern Uplands, St Mary's Loch is the largest natural body of freshwater in the Borders Region. The Southern Upland Way long distance path follows its eastern shoreline while the famous Tibbie Shiels Inn at its southern end is a popular destination for anglers, walkers and campers.*

ARGYLL, THE TROSSACHS AND FIFE

Loch Finlaggan
Loch Awe
Loch Lomond
Loch Ard
Loch Vennacher
Loch Katrine
Loch Lubnaig
Loch Earn
Loch Leven

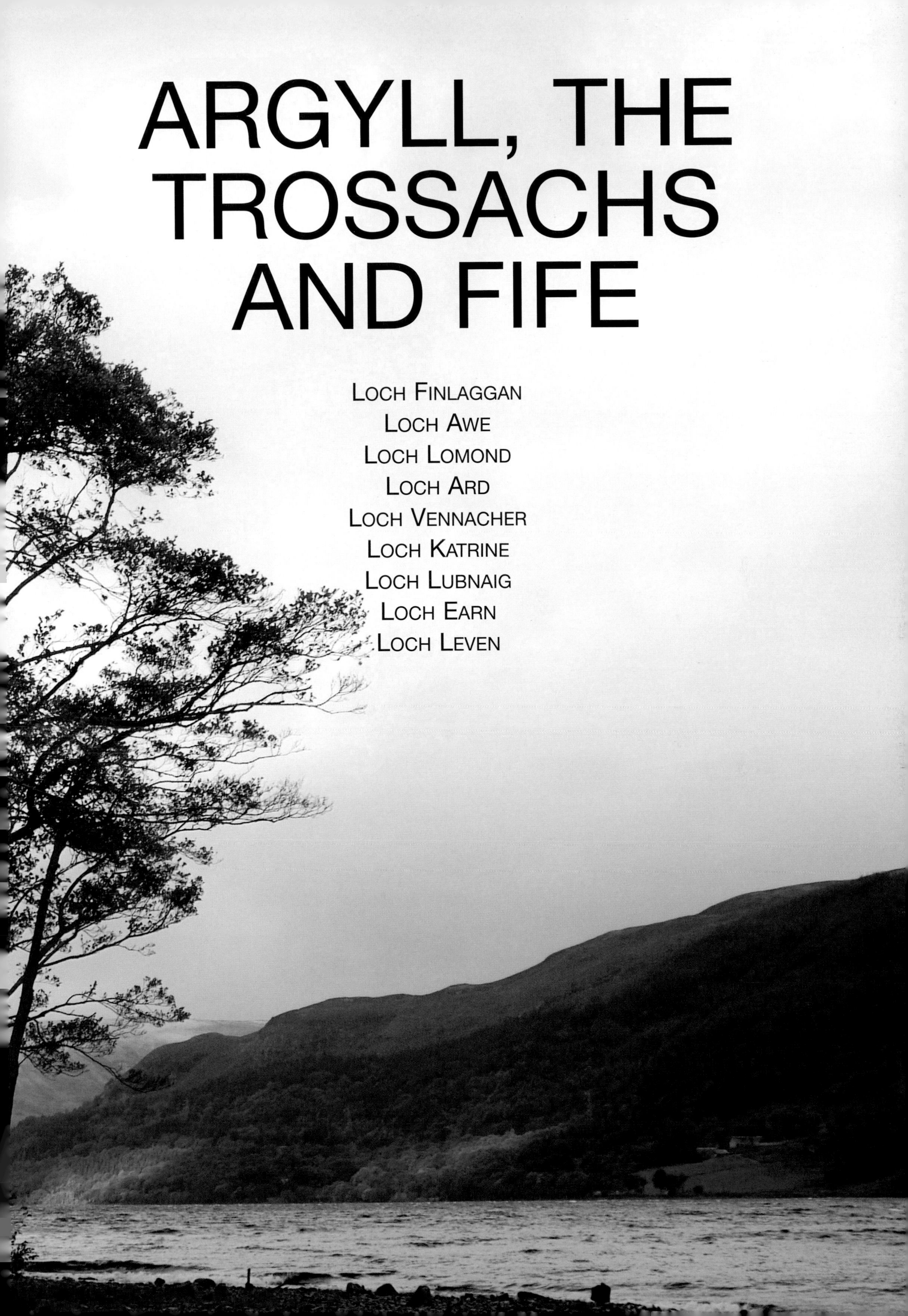

LOCH FINLAGGAN

LOCH FINLAGGAN
VITAL STATISTICS
Max. length: 1.25mi
Surface area: 0.4mi²
Average depth: 33ft
Max. depth: 65ft
Water volume: 2.3
billion gallons

ORDNANCE
SURVEY 1: 50,000
LANDRANGER MAP
No. 60

Despite its small size and remoteness Loch Finlaggan has played a big part in Scottish history. Found in the lochan-littered landscape of the northern part of the island of Islay, the loch and its tiny islands were once the home and centre of government of Clan Donald, whose chiefs were the powerful Lords of the Isles in the 14th and 15th centuries.

HISTORY

Recent archaeological excavations near Loch Finlaggan by Channel 4's *Time Team* have discovered flint tools, animal bones, standing stone and a burial chamber dating from the Early Bronze Age around 4,000 years ago. Other standing stones and hillforts, or duns, can be found at several locations near the loch. There are three islands in the loch: one is a crannog or man-made island found in the south; the other two are Eilean Mor and Eilean na Comhairle at the northern end. The early Christian missionary St Findlugan built a chapel on Eilean Mor in the late 6th century AD before Viking invaders, attracted by Islay's fertile soils, mineral deposits and accessibility to the sea, arrived on the scene in the 10th century.

In the 14th century the all-powerful Clan Donald, descended from the 12th century prince, Somerled, established their home and administration centre on the two islands in the loch. From here their chiefs, the Lords of the Isles, ruled their Gaelic kingdom that stretched from the Mull of Kintyre to the Isle of Lewis.

The first Lord of the Isles was John who ruled from 1329 to 1387 and the dynasty ended in 1493 during the rule of the fourth Lord, John II, when all the lands of the Lords of the Isles were forfeited to the Scottish crown. The title Lord of the Isles was annexed to the British Crown in 1542 and is now one of the titles of the present Prince of Wales.

Formed in 1984 to preserve the historic ruins on Eilean Mor and Eilean na Comhairle, the Finlaggan Trust now runs a small museum and interpretive centre on the north shore of Loch Finlaggan. For more details contact: The Finlaggan Trust, The Cottage, Ballygrant, Isle of Islay, Argyll PA45 7QL or visit: www.finlaggan.com

NATURAL HISTORY

First and foremost Islay is famous for its birdlife which includes 200 different species of bird, of which around 100 breed on the island. The fertile limestone farmland around Loch Finlaggan are regular haunts of lapwing, curlew, hen harrier and corncrake while in the

winter months around 50,000 Greenland barnacle and white-fronted geese descend on the island. Red deer and mountain hare are a common sight in the hills to the north of the loch. For more information about the island's wildlife visit: www.islayinfo.cm/wildlife or The Islay Natural History Trust, Port Charlotte, Isle of Islay PA48 7TX. Website: www.islaynaturalhistory,org

WALKING AND CYCLING

From the small car park at the Finlaggan Trust's centre at the north end of the loch, a forestry track leads to coniferous woodland containing the tiny Loch Airigh nan Caisteal. Here there is an unroofed shieling hut which was probably used on a seasonal basis by people tending animals on upland pastures. Another track leads northwards to Loch Staoisha and the remote hills and forests of northern Islay.

ANGLING AND BOAT HIRE

There are many freshwater lochs on the Islay Estates where wild brown trout can be caught. Loch Finlaggan fishes well through the season between 15 March

and 30 September, although May-July are considered the best. For information on permits and boat hire contact Islay Estates Office (Tel +44 (0) 1496 810221 or visit: www.islayestatcs.com)

TOURIST INFORMATION AND ACCOMMODATION

Bowmore Tourist Information Centre, The Square, Bowmore, Isle of Islay, Argyll PA43 7JP. Tel. +44 (0) 8707 200617. Website: www.visit.scotland.com

Above and below *Approached via a short but boggy causeway from the Finlaggan Trust's visitor centre, the island of Eilean Mor was once the centre of an extensive kingdom ruled over by the Clan Donald and their chief, the Lord of the Isles, from 1329 to 1493. Stretching from Kintyre to the Isle of Lewis the lands and islands of these powerful rulers were forfeited to the Scottish crown following wars on the mainland. The last Lord of the Isles, John II, died in exile in a Paisley monastery in 1503.*

LOCH AWE

**LOCH AWE
VITAL STATISTICS**
Max. length: 25mi
Surface area: 14.9mi²
Average depth: 164ft
Max. depth: 311ft
Water volume: 424
billion gallons

**ORDNANCE
SURVEY 1: 50,000
LANDRANGER MAPS
NOS. 50/55**

Below *Now popular with anglers and wild campers, the northern end of Loch Awe was once served by a regular steamboat passenger service that connected with trains from Glasgow at Loch Awe Pier. The regular daily service down to Ford, at the southern end, first called at Taychreggan, now known as North Port, on the west shore, before making the short crossing to Port Sonachan on the east shore. Sadly this service is now a fading memory and the only alternative between these two places is a 38-mile car journey around the narrow and winding perimeter road via Ford.*

Once a sea loch, or fjord, shaped by a glacier during the Ice Age, Loch Awe is the third largest (by surface area) freshwater loch in Scotland and is also the longest. The build-up of glacial debris at its southern end eventually blocked drainage to the sea and the loch overflowed at its northern end through the Pass of Brander to Loch Etive. Raised beaches seen along the loch today are a reminder of the time when, tens of thousands of years ago, Loch Awe was still a sea loch.

Although there are over 50 islands on Loch Awe, some of these are crannogs or man-made islands dating from 500BC onwards. The largest of the loch's natural islands are found at its northern end with Inishail being the largest – the latter is the site of a 10th century church while Fraoch Eilean and, to the south, Innis Chonnell, are the sites of ruined castles.

HISTORY

Apart from a few chambered cairns found on the west side of the loch, little is known of prehistoric man's activities around the loch. However, dating from the period between 500BC and the 14th century, there are at least 15 known crannogs dotted around the shores of the loch. These offshore homes, safe from natural predators and constructed of stones, trunks and branches, were built by farmers who worked the rich glacial soils alongside the loch.

Fought in 1308, the Battle of the Pass of Brander at the northern end of Loch Awe was a bloody turning point in the Wars of Scottish Independence. Aiming to ambush the army of Robert Bruce in the narrow confines of the pass, the army of the Lord of Argyll, Alexander MacDougall, was taken by surprise by Black Douglas's Highlanders who attacked then in the rear from the heights of Ben Cruachan. Argyll's men suffered heavy casualties as they tried to retreat across the loch.

Of the four castles located around the loch Kilchurn Castle is by far the most important and largest. It was built on what was then a small island at the northern end of the loch by Sir Colin

Right *Dating from the period between 500BC to the 14th century there are at least 15 known crannogs, or small man-made islands, dotted around the shores of the loch. A good example can be seen at Ardanaiseig just offshore from the grounds of a hotel.*

Campbell, the 1st Lord of Glenorchy, in the mid-15th century. Access to it was originally via a causeway but falling water levels in the 19th century led to it losing its island status. Home to the Campbells for 400 years, the castle was considerably extended by Sir John Campbell in the 1690s when he built extensive barracks capable of housing 200 soldiers. During the Jacobite Rebellions of 1715 and 1745 the castle was used as a Government garrison but by the end of this period the Campbells had moved to Taymouth and the castle fell into disuse. Its substantial ruins, reached along a footpath from the A85 near the River Orchy, are now in the care of Historic Scotland.

The three other ruined castles on Loch Awe are on Fraoch Eilean (13th century), Innis Chonnell (11th century) and at Fincharn (13th century). While the two former castles can be reached by boat the latter, at the southern end of the loch, is on private land.

At the north end of the loch the narrow Pass of Brander has for centuries provided a strategically important route linking the west coast of Scotland and the Highlands with the Lowlands via Strathyre (see pages 50-53). The narrow confines of the pass were also used by the Callander & Oban Railway which opened throughout in 1880. Perched on a ledge below the slopes of Ben Cruachan the railway has always been at the mercy of rockfalls. To warn train drivers of impending danger a series of mechanical 'trip' wires linked to semaphore signals run for over four miles alongside the track as it wends its way through the Pass of Brander. In theory any rockfall will immediately trigger the signals to stand at danger but a serious incident along this stretch in June 2010 calls into doubt its integrity.

Above *About halfway down the loch's eastern shore lies the tiny island of Innis Errich. Here there are remains of a 15th or 16th century chapel and a burial ground which contains a table-tomb in memory of William McAllum who died in 1732.*

The coming of the railway to the northern end of Loch Awe also led to a regular steamboat service along the loch. The heyday of these steamers was during the Victorian and Edwardian eras when many houses with private piers were built along the loch by wealthy owners. At this time communications along the loch were better by water than by road and from 1895 to 1918 the *TSS Caledonia* ran a regular public passenger service between Loch Awe Pier and Ford via Taychreggan and Port Sonachan – the 26-mile journey being completed in a leisurely two hours and ten minutes. Other privately owned steamers such as *The Countess of Breadalbane* and the *Growley* also saw service into the 1920s and 1930s. Passenger ferries on Loch Awe sadly ended in the early 1950s and their revival along this beautiful stretch of water in the future is only a pipedream at the moment.

By the 1930s the Forestry Commission, set up by the Government after World War I, had become a major player around Loch Awe. Two of the largest commercial forests in the UK can be found on either side of the loch – on the west shore is Inverleiver Forest which was purchased by HM Officer of Woods in 1907 while on the east shore stands Eredine Forest. The latter was originally a hill farm that was purchased by the Commission in the 1930s and planted mainly with Norway and Sitka spruce. Today the Commission is the largest employer around Loch Awe.

In the latter half of the 20th century the waters of Loch Awe were also harnessed to produce electricity. The smallest of the two hydro-electric schemes is in the Pass of Brander where the River Awe has been dammed and its waters fed through a small conventional turbine power station before outflowing to the sea in Loch Etive. Further east along the pass is the important Cruachan pumped storage sheme which was completed n 1965. One of only four such power stations in the UK, water is pumped by reversible turbines from Loch Awe to a reservoir 1,299ft above on Ben Cruachan during the night when electricity is cheap. During periods of peak demand the water is released from the reservoir and allowed to flow back down to Loch Awe via the generating hall located in the heart of the mountain. Visits to the 'hollow mountain' generating hall can be made from the Cruachan Power Station Visitor Centre alongside the A85 in the Pass of Brander. For more information visit: www.visitcruachan.co.uk

MYTHS AND LEGENDS

The sighting of serpent-like creature in Loch Awe was documented by the famous 16th century Scottish cartographer Timothy Pont. Apparently this so-called 'giant eel' frightened fishermen away from the loch but there have never been any recorded sightings of it since then.

NATURAL HISTORY

Located on the west shore of Loch Awe close to the forestry village of Dalavich, the Dalavich Oakwoods are one of the largest unique remnants of the native Caledonian Forest that once covered the western seaboard of Scotland. Much of the 395 acres are protected as a Site of Special Scientific Interest (SSSI) and are home to a wide range of plant and wildlife. As well as red deer, roe deer and red squirrel there is also the rare and elusive wild cat and pine marten. Birdlife

Left *The small island of Innis Chonnell lies a short distance off the east shore of the loch opposite the village of Dalavich. Probably dating from the 11th century, the castle was the main stronghold of the Campbells until the building of Kilchurn Castle at the top end of the loch by Sir Colin Campbell in the mid-15th century.*

is prolific with the whole range of northwestern woodland bird species to be found here - from woodpeckers, dipper, finch, blue, long-tailed, great and coal tits, the tiny gold crest and tree creeper to the rarer pied flycatcher and redstart. The woodland is also home to the rare pearl-bordered fritillary. The Forestry Commission's Dalavich Oakwood Trail starts at the Barnaline Interpretation Centre one mile north of Dalavich.

The clear waters of Loch Awe support a thriving fish population, in particular the wild brown trout. No doubt attracted by this plentiful food source the rare osprey is now making a comeback to this part of Scotland - in 2010 a pair made a nest on a mobile phone tower overlooking a fish farm opposite the Cruachan Power Station.

WALKING AND CYCLING

Walkers and cyclists are well catered for around Loch Awe. Numerous woodland trails abound both in Inverliever Forest on the west shore and Eredine Forest on the east shore. In particular there are waymarked trails for families in the Dalavich Oakwoods (see NATURAL HISTORY) and nearby Avich Falls. For off-road cyclists the Inverliever Cycle Trail, the Two Lochs Cycle Trail and the Kilmaha/New York Cycle Trail can all be found in Inverliever Forest. On-road cycling is a joy as there is little traffic on the B840 along the east shore or on the minor road along the west shore. Route 78 of the National Cycle Network follows the latter route.

CANOEING AND KAYAKING

Canoes can be hired from Loch Awe Boats (see right) at Ardbrecknish. The loch is popular with canoeists, wild campers and fishermen who can be seen in quite large numbers during the

summer months camping by the east shore of the loch alongside the B840.

ANGLING AND BOAT HIRE

All fishing on Loch Awe is governed by a Protection Order granted in 1992 and enforced by the Loch Awe Improvement Association. With its many bays the loch is famous for its wild brown trout and has broken the British rod-caught record many times in recent years. Fishing is by permit only with separate tickets for trout, salmon, pike and coarse fish - permits are available at Loch Awe Stores and the Tight Line pub in Lochawe village, Loch Awe Boats at Ardbrecknish and in tackle shops in Oban. Boat hire is available from Loch Awe Boats, The Boat House, Ardbrecknish, By Dalmally, Argyll PA33 1BH (Tel +44 (0) 1866 833 256. Website: www.loch-awe.com/boats

TOURIST INFORMATION AND ACCOMMODATION

Lochgilphead Tourist Information Centre, Lochnell Street, Lochgilphead, Argyll PA31 8JL. Tel +44 (0) 8452 255121
Website: www.visitscotland.com

Above *Located at the northern end of Loch Awe, Kilchurn Castle was originally built on a small island by Sir Colin Campbell, the 1st Lord of Glenorchy, in the mid-15th century. Access to it was originally via a causeway but falling water levels in the 19th century led to it losing its island status. Its substantial ruins, reached along a footpath from the A85 near the River Orchy outflow, are now in the care of Historic Scotland.*

Below *Close to Kilchurn Castle and overlooked by the misty peak of Beinn Eunaich this bridge carries the Glasgow to Oban railway across the mouth of the River Orchy at the northern end of Loch Awe.*

LOCH LOMOND
VITAL STATISTICS
Max. length: 24mi
Surface area: 27.5mi²
Average depth: 121ft
Max. depth: 623ft
Water volume: 577
billion gallons

ORDNANCE
SURVEY 1: 50,000
LANDRANGER MAP
NO. 56

LOCH LOMOND

Loch Lomond is the largest freshwater lake (by surface area) in Great Britain and is the second largest (by volume of water) in Scotland. The southern end of the loch is crossed by the Highland Boundary Fault, the geological division between Highland and Lowland Scotland formed hundreds of millions of years ago by movements in the earth's crust.

Now part of the Loch Lomond and the Trossachs National Park, the loch contains 30 islands including Inchmurrin which is the largest on any freshwater lake in the British Isles – the island has a hotel and a naturist club. The loch's proximity to Glasgow, Scotland's largest city, led to its popularity as a destination for daytrippers in the 19th century.

The loch is fed by numerous burns and rivers – notably the River Falloch –

mainly at its northern end where there is more rainfall. At its southern end the loch outflows to the Firth of Clyde and the sea via the River Leven. Fed by waters from Loch Sloy, hydro-electricity is generated at the Inveruglas power station on the western shore while, since 1971, up to 100 million gallons of water are taken from the loch each day to boost water supplies in central Scotland.

HISTORY

Loch Lomond's shores have been inhabited for thousands of years. Numerous burial cairns, standing stones and cup and ring markings dating from the New Stone Age can be found at various locations around the loch. The later Iron Age is also well represented by hilltop forts or duns such as those found

Right *Moored near Balloch next to the reopened Balloch Steam Slipway, the* Maid of the Loch *was the last paddle steamer built in Britain. Launched in 1953, she plied up and down the loch until 1981. Following restoration this historic ship is now a floating restaurant*

at Arroychymore Point and Strathcashell Point on the eastern shore north of Balmaha.

During their occupation of Britain the Romans penetrated Scotland, pushing back the Caledoni tribes north of Antonine's Wall which was built between the Forth and the Clyde. Remains of the most westerly fort on the wall at Old Kilpatrick, a few miles southeast of Balloch, can still be seen today. By the 3rd century AD the Romans had gone home and were replaced in Southern Scotland by the Kingdom of Strathclyde.

By the early 6th century AD early Christian missionaries from Ireland had reached the shores of Loch Lomond, among them St Kessog who became Scotland's patron saint before St Andrew. Kessog brought Christianity to the area around Luss, on the loch's western shore, making his headquarters on Monk's Island or Inchtavannach until he was martyred in 520AD.

Following the Norman invasion of Britain in 1066 the Earldom of Lennox, including the loch and what is now Dumbartonshire, was created. Existing until 1748 the long list of Earls included two (Lord Darnley and Earl Duncan) who were to fall from grace and who were beheaded.

Loch Lomond has seen its fair share of bloody fighting but the most dreadful event occurred in 1263 when the Vikings, under King Haakon IV of Norway, raided the loch's shores in a surprise attack, destroying townships and murdering their inhabitants. The ingenious Vikings had gained access to the landlocked loch by sailing up Long Long to Arrochar and then dragging their galleys over the narrow isthmus to Tarbet. After having laid waste to the shores of Loch Lomond they sailed south down the River Leven to the Firth of Clyde where their fleet awaited them. Unfortunately for the Vikings their fleet

was driven ashore at Largs during a storm. Here they were engaged in an inconclusive battle with Scottish forces led by King Alexander III.

The Scottish clans that lived and fought around the loch were Lennox, MacGregor, Colquhoun, Graham, MacFarlane and Buchanan. To the west of the loch at its southern end, Glen Fruin was the scene of the last clan battle in Scotland, fought between the MacGregors and Colquhouns in 1603.

Immortalised by Sir Walter Scott in his novels, Rob Roy MacGregor (1671–1734) was one of the most colourful local figures of this period and his cave, believed to have been previously used as a refuge by Robert the Bruce in 1306, can be seen alongside the West Highland Way on the eastern shore opposite Wallace's Isle near Inveruglas.

Loch Lomond has also been immortalised in a famous song that was first published around 1841. Its words, famous the world-over, are attributed to a Scottish soldier who apparently wrote them while on his way home after the failed 1745 Rebellion:

> Oh, ye'll tak' the high road, and I'll tak' the low road,
> And I'll be in Scotland afore ye;
> But me and my true love will never meet again
> On the bonnie, bonnie banks o' Loch Lomond

For centuries the loch has been an important line of communication between the western Highlands and central Lowlands. From the 16th century the tracks along its shores were heavily used by cattle drovers en route to the important market at Crieff and later at Falkirk. Cattle were also swum across the loch at its narrower points.

The loch's proximity to the growing industrial city of Glasgow soon led to its popularity as a destination for daytrippers in the 19th century. The first loch steamer, the *Marion*, arrived in 1818 and operated a service from Balloch to Inversnaid. Soon, other steamers had arrived including *The Lady of the Lake* and piers were built around the loch at various locations.

Public transport to the loch was much improved in 1851 when the Dumbarton & Balloch Joint Railway opened its line up the Vale of Leven to Balloch Pier where visitors could transfer on to the Loch Lomond steamers for a day's cruise up the loch. On nationalisation of Britain's transport system in 1948 the loch's steamers came under the control of British Railways – the last of these was the *Maid of the Loch* which was introduced in 1953 and continued in service until 1981 – by then the era of the loch steamers had ended although the *Maid* still survives as a floating restaurant at Balloch. Balloch Pier station also closed with the railway being cut back to a new station in Balloch.

Railways also came to the northern end of the loch in 1894 when the West Highland Railway was opened between Glasgow and Fort William. Still open today there are stations at Arrochar & Tarbet and Ardlui.

Despite the proximity to Glasgow, modern development around the loch is minimal apart from at Balloch where the Lomond Shores shopping mall, part-financed by the EU, and Sealife Aquarium, were opened in 2002.

Right *Between Balmaha and Inverarnan the quieter eastern shore of Loch Lomond, seen here at Craigie Fort near Balmaha, is traversed by the West Highland Way long distance path that runs between Milngavie, north of Glasgow, to Fort William.*

NATURAL HISTORY

With some of the finest scenery in Europe, Loch Lomond is deservedly located in Scotland's first national park - its full name is Loch Lomond & The Trossachs National Park. Established in 2002 it is the fourth largest in the British Isles with a total area of 729 square miles, includes 21 Munros (of which the nearest to the loch is Ben Lomond (3,194ft), two forest parks (Queen Elizabeth and Argyll) and over 50 special nature conservation sites. The Loch Lomond National Nature Reserve lies in the southeast corner of the loch and includes important tracts of native deciduous woodlands and wetlands.

The nature reserve also includes four of the loch's islands - Bucinch, Clairinsh, Inclonaig and Inchcailloch, the latter reached by ferry during the summer from Balmaha - each supporting rich, mature oak woodland. Bluebells and wild garlic carpet the woodlands in the spring when migrant warblers, flycatchers and redsatarts start to return.

The shores around the loch are home to a wide diversity of plant and animal life - 25% of Britain's wild plants have been recorded in the area while there are around 200 different species of birds, native and migratory, to be seen at various times of the year. Highlights include golden eagle, peregrine falcon, osprey, ptarmigan and capercaillie - the latter breeding on two of the more secluded islands. The wetlands around the mouth of the River Endrick play host to a good number of wildfowl, including wigeon, mallard and teal, in the winter while numbers of visiting greylag, pink-footed and Greenland white-fronted geese can often rise to 2,000 - 3,000 birds.

Wild mammals found around the loch include wild cat, deer and ferral goat while a herd of wallaby, introduced by Lady Arran Colquhoun in the 1920s, still survive on Inchconnachan island.

There are about 14 different species of fish to be found in Loch Lomond - the most important are the salmon and sea trout which swim up the River Leven from the sea in search of their spawning grounds each year. The most unusual fish in southern end of the loch is the powan which is a rare type of freshwater herring that became trapped in Loch Lomond (then a sea loch) during the last ice age and, as the water de-salinated, adapted to its new environment.

WALKING, CLIMBING AND CYCLING

Away from the busy A82 which hugs the loch's western shore, the area surrounding Loch Lomond is a paradise for walkers and climbers. The quieter eastern shore is only accessible by car at two points - via a minor road between Balmaha and Rowardennan and at Inversnaid, the latter reached via a circuitous route through Aberfoyle. Both of these lochside locations have car parks and are excellent starting points for walkers along the West Highland Way or for the more strenuous climb to the top of Ben Lomond. The 153-mile West Highland Way is a long distance traffic-free path that runs between Milngavie, north of Glasgow, to Fort William and is used by about 85,000 people each year. Its route along the east shore of Loch Lomond follows the line of an old drovers road and can be broken up into more manageable 7-mile sections

allowing a full day's walk with a return journey. The sections are: Balmaha - Rowardennan; Rowardennan - Inversnaid; Inversnaid - Inverarnan - there are no access roads to the path on the latter section which is also popular with wild campers. Infrequent but timetabled passenger ferries operate across the loch during the summer months between Inversnaid and Inveruglas and between Rowardennan and Inverbeg.

For cyclists, National Cycle Network Route 7 passes through Balloch at the southern end of the loch.

CANOEING, KAYAKING AND SAILING

With its numerous islands Loch Lomond is a popular location for water sports enthusiasts. For canoeists the loch can be accessed from the east shore at Milarrochy Bay, Sallochy car park or at Rowardennan. Access from the west shore is at Luss car park, Tarbet car park and Inveruglas. From the south it can be accessed at Balloch from Duncan Mills Memorial Slipway or at Duck Bay. Note that wild camping is now banned from the eastern shore between Balmaha and Rowardennan in response to a growing problem of litter and anti-social behaviour.

Sailors are catered for by the Loch Lomond Sailing Club which is based on the east shore near Milarrochy, north of Balmaha. For more details visit: www.lochlomondsc.org

There are three official slipways: Milarrochy Bay, near Balmaha; Drumkinnon Bay, Balloch; River Leven, Balloch. The latter is unsuitable for large boats.

Above *Rowardennan, on the east shore of Loch Lomond, is at the end of the minor road from Balmaha. Here, there is a car park for walkers, a hotel and a ferry service to Inverbeg on the west shore. The Rowardennan estate was bought after World War II by the National Land Fund and is now part of the Ben Lomond National Memorial Park. The Park and this memorial were dedicated in 1996 as a tribute to those who gave their lives in the service of their country.*

Above *Known as 'Wee Peter', this statue can be seen in the loch just offshore at Aldochlay south of Luss. It was erected in 1890 by a local stonemason who had found it in a London scrapyard.*

BOAT AND SEAPLANE TRIPS

Several companies offer a variety of cruises on Loch Lomond. These include:
Cruise Loch Lomond Ltd, Tarbet
Tel. +44 (0) 1301 702356
Website: www.cruiselochlomondltd.com
Sweeney's Cruises, Balloch
Tel. +44 (0) 1389 752376
Website: www.sweeney.uk.com

Loch Lomond Seaplanes operate tour and charter flights in their Cessna 208 Caravan from Loch Lomond and from their terminal in Glasgow City Centre. For more information visit:
www.lochlomondseaplanes.com

ANGLING AND BOAT HIRE

Loch Lomond provides some of the best game and coarse fishing available in the UK. Salmon and sea trout return up the River Leven into the southern end of the loch, while brown and rainbow trout, pike, perch, roach, chub and dace offer a wide variety for anglers.

Fishing on the loch is managed by the Loch Lomond Angling Improvement Association (LLAIA). For more details visit: www.lochlomondangling.com

Permits are available from the LLAIA

or from various outlets in Ardlui, Luss, Balloch and Balmaha.

Boat hire is available from Macfarlane & Son at Balmaha Boatyard
Tel. +44 (0) 1360 870214
Website: www.balmahaboatyard.co.uk

TOURIST INFORMATION AND ACCOMMODATION

Balloch Tourist Information Centre, Balloch Road, Balloch, Dunbartonshire G83 8LQ. Tel +44 (0) 8707 200 607
Website: www.visitscottishheartlands.com

Below *The largest island on Loch Lomond and the largest on any freshwater body in the British Isles is Inchmurrin. Originally the Duke of Montrose's deer park, the island is now home to a hotel, holiday chalets and a naturists club.*

LOCH ARD
VITAL STATISTICS
Max. length: 1.86mi
Surface area: 0.58mi²
Average depth: 56ft
Max. depth: 98ft
Water volume: 5.6
billion gallons

ORDNANCE
SURVEY 1: 50,000
LANDRANGER MAP
NO. 57

LOCH ARD

Below *Wreathed in mist, the still and sheltered waters of Loch Ard offer ideal conditions for canoeing and kayaking. The surrounding vast tracts of Loch Ard Forest are not only a haven for plant and wild life, but also a popular destination for walkers and cyclists.*

Considered to be the source of the River Forth, Loch Ard is a small, picturesque and sheltered loch set among forests in the Loch Lomond & The Trossachs National Park. The largest of the several small islands (one a man-made crannog) is Eilean Gorm. The loch's sheltered location makes it ideal for canoeing, kayaking and sailing while the vast area of Loch Ard Forest (part of the Queen Elizabeth Forest Park) to the south is interlaced with a network of mountain bike trails and walks.

HISTORY

A crannog, or man-made island, in the southwest corner of the loch dates from the Iron Age, while the small island of Dundochil off the south shore is the site of an early 15th century castle built as a hunting lodge by Murdoch Stewart, Duke of Albany. Murdoch was Regent of Scotland while James I of Scotland was being held by the English. Unfortunately for Murdoch, he was accused of poor government by James on his release from prison and was executed in 1425. His estates around Loch Ard were seized and became part of the Earldom of Monteith. Although primarily a hunting forest other activities included farming and iron production – the latter smelted by charcoal burning made possible by the plentiful supplies of local timber.

The publication of Sir Walter Scott's novels *Waverley* (1814) and *Rob Roy* (1817) – both of which mention Loch Ard – led to a growing public interest in the area. The Trossachs also became

famous when Queen Victoria opened the new water supply to Glasgow from nearby Loch Katrine (see pages 44-49) in 1859. Following a private visit to nearby Invertrossachs in 1869, The Trossachs became one of her favourite Scottish destinations. Following the end of World War I the Forestry Commission was created to provide a strategic resource of timber and is now one of the biggest employers in the area around Loch Ard. Today, Loch Ard Forest is a popular destination for walkers and cyclists.

MYTHS AND LEGENDS

The first part of this story is fact, the second half is legend. Born in 1644, Rev Robert Kirk was a minister in nearby Aberfoyle and, as well as translating the *Book of Psalms* into Gaelic, he wrote *The Secret Commonwealth of Elves, Fauns and Faeries*. For years his daily exercise consisted of a walk to Doon Hill and back, but in May 1692 he never returned home. Legend has it that the Faeries, angry at the disclosures in his book, seized him and took him to their underworld. His imprisoned spirit is said to be inside the lone pine tree that now stands at the top of the hill.

NATURAL HISTORY

Managed by the Forestry Commission, the enormous tracts of Loch Ard Forest stretch from Aberfoyle in the east to the eastern slopes of the Ben Lomond Memorial Park in the west. The forest, with its many lochans, is home to a wide range of wildlife including red and roe deer, red squirrel, capercaillie, woodpecker, blackcock and barn owl. Rare plants and fungi also abound in this man-made wilderness.

The Forestry Commission's David Marshall Lodge Visitor Centre near Aberfoyle is the main centre for wildlife information and observation and has several live webcams documenting bird (including osprey) and animal life in the area. For more information contact the Centre on +44 (0) 1877 382258 or visit: www.forestry.gov.uk

WALKING AND CYCLING

With its 16 miles of waymarked routes Loch Ard Forest is a paradise for walkers and cyclists. There are five different cycling trails, suitable for all abilities, ranging from two to ten miles long. The three start points for the Loch Ard Family Sculpture Trails are at the main forest car park in Aberfoyle, Milton car park at the east end of Loch Ard and in Kinlochard village at the west end of the loch. Along the trails are sound posts, a wildlife hide with chainsaw sculptures and unusual seats and shelters. For more information contact the recreation team of Cowal & Trossachs Forest District Council (Tel. +44 (0) 1877 382383).

TOURIST INFORMATION AND ACCOMMODATION

Aberfoyle Tourist Information Centre, Main Street, Aberfoyle, Stirlingshire FK8 3UQ. Tel. Tel. +44 (0) 8452 255121 Website: www.visitscotland.com

ANGLING AND BOAT HIRE

Managed by the Forestry Commission, Loch Ard contains large pike, brown trout and perch – the current Scottish record for the latter (4lb 14oz) was caught in the loch in 1989. Fishing is by permit from boats or bank. Permits can be obtained from the newsagent, Alskeath Hotel or the Forest Hills Hotel, all in Kinlochard.

CANOEING AND KAYAKING

Loch Ard's sheltered location makes it an ideal spot for canoeing and kayaking. The Macdonald Forest Hills Hotel at Kinlochard organise watersports activities on the loch – these include canoeing, kayaking, dinghy sailing and boat hire. For more details contact the hotel on +44 (0) 844 879 9057 or visit: www.macdonaldhotels.co.uk/foresthills

LOCH VENNACHER
VITAL STATISTICS
Max. length: 3.7mi
Surface area: 1.9mi²
Average depth: 65ft
Max. depth: 108ft
Water volume: 21
billion gallons

ORDNANCE
SURVEY 1: 50,000
LANDRANGER MAP
NO. 57

LOCH VENACHER

Set in the Loch Lomond & The Trossachs National Park, Loch Venacher is fed by water at its western end from Loch Achray via the Black Water and outflows via Eas Gobhain to the River Teith at Callander. To the east of the loch are numerous glacial features such as eskers and rocks dumped by retreating glaciers over 10,000 years ago.

HISTORY
Nearby Callander occupies a once-important stategic position to the south of the narrow Pass of Leny. Evidence of an early Stone Age farming community dating back 6,000 years was recently uncovered near Callander. Pictish tribes later inhabited the area around Loch Venacher - dating from this period is Dunmore Fort, a series of earth ridges on the top of a hill halfway between the loch and Callander. Nearer the town are the remains of a short-lived Roman fort at Bochastle built during the governorship of Sallustus Lucullus around 85AD. The remains of a temporary Roman marching camp were also discovered nearby in 1949.

Set in the middle of Rob Roy MacGregor country (see pages 44-49), the town of Callander was built on land originally owned by the Drummond Estate, seized by the government after the 1745 Jacobite Rebellion. Made popular in the early 19th century by Wordsworth and Sir Walter Scott, Callander was placed firmly on the tourist map with the coming of the railway in 1858. The visit of Queen Victoria to Invertrossachs

Below *To the north of Loch Venacher is Ben Ledi, the most southerly of Scotland's 'Bens'. A popular destination for anglers, the loch has a large native population of wild brown trout sustained by a wide variety of aquatic and terrestrial insects. The loch also has an abundant stock of pike and these can be fished by bank or boat. Fly fishing for pike is also popular with a 42lb beast being caught in 2002. As with other pike caught here the 13½ lb specimen seen below right was returned unharmed to the loch.*

House on the south shore of Loch Venacher in 1869 stamped the final seal of approval on the area. Although the railway sadly closed in 1965, tourism is still a major contributor to the local economy.

NATURAL HISTORY

The south shore of the loch is covered by woodland on the lower northern slopes of the Menteith Hills. To the west of this is Achray Forest, itself forming part of the Queen Elizabeth Forest Park, a large area of woodland famed for its diverse plant and animal life. To the north of the loch lies the peak of Ben Ledi (2,883ft), its lower slopes home to red deer and its crags home to the golden eagle. The mountain is best reached from the car park in the Pass of Leny.

CANOEING AND KAYAKING

Access is from several lochside car parks on the A821 along the northern shore. Canoe and kayak trips are also organised by Trossachs Leisure (see ANGLING AND BOAT HIRE).

WALKING AND CYCLING

The wooded south shore of the loch is criss-crossed by numerous tracks and paths, some leading west to Loch Achray, Loch Katrine and The Trossachs, while to south they lead over the Menteith Hills to the Lake of Menteith and its historic island of Inchmahome. Route 7 of the National Cycle Network runs along the southern shore of the loch and continues through Achray Forest to Aberfoyle and is considered

to be one of the most scenic sections of the entire NCN. All of these routes can be accessed from the car park near the water works at the eastern end of the loch.

ANGLING AND BOAT HIRE

Loch Venacher is famous for its large pike and wild brown trout while the number of sea trout and salmon caught in recent years has significantly increased. Permits and boat hire are available from Trossachs Leisure on the north shore. For more details Tel. +44 (0) 1877 330011 or visit: www.trossachs-leisure.co.uk

TOURIST INFORMATION AND ACCOMMODATION

Callander Tourist Information Centre, 10 Ancaster Square, Callander, Perthshire FK17 8ED. Tel. +44 (0)8452 255121
Website: www.visitscotland.com
or www.incallander.co.uk

LOCH KATRINE

LOCH KATRINE VITAL STATISTICS
Max. length: 8mi
Surface area: 5.9mi^2
Average depth: 246ft
Max. depth: 475ft
Water volume: 252 billion gallons

ORDNANCE SURVEY 1: 50,000 LANDRANGER MAPS NOS. 56/57

One of the largest lochs in the Trossachs, Loch Katrine runs the length of Strath Gartney which was formed by the scouring of glaciers during the last Ice Age (c. two million years ago – c. 11,500 years ago).

The loch is owned by Scottish Water and is the main reservoir for Glasgow and its environs. Up to 50 million gallons of water per day flow from the loch along two 26-mile aqueducts to a water treatment plant at Milngavie. Loch Katrine is kept topped up by water fed through tunnels from Loch Arklet, to the west, and Glen Finglas Reservoir, to the north. When the loch is full any water outflows through sluices its eastern end to the River Teith at Callander via Loch Achray and Loch Venachar.

There are three small islands on Loch Katrine - Eilean Molach at the eastern end, and Black Isle and Factor's Island to the west.

HISTORY

It is thought that Loch Katrine was named after the 'caterans' or cattle rustlers that once inhabited the Trossachs. The most famous of these highland cattle rustlers was Rob Roy MacGregor who was born at Glen Gyle at the western end of the loch in 1671. This famous Scottish folk hero and outlaw joined the Jacobite rising of 1715 and was wounded at the Battle of Glen Shiel in 1719 when Government forces defeated a combined army of Jacobites and Spaniards. Rob Roy later settled down and became a successful cattleman until bad luck befell him and, unable to pay his creditors, he lost everything. His lands were seized by the Duke of Montrose and, as a result, he was branded an outlaw. Following years of bloody feuding with the duke, in which Rob Roy imprisoned his factor on an island on Loch Katrine, he was finally caught and imprisoned in 1722. He was later pardoned and died at Balquhidder in 1734.

Loch Katrine is also famous for its association with Sir Walter Scott and his famous poem *The Lady of the Lake* which was published in 1810. Based on Arthurian legend and set in the Trossachs, the poem became such a hit that his fans thronged to the region in their thousands. Along with the loch itself one of the magical places referred to in his poem was Eilean Molach or Ellen's Isle, at the eastern end - to this day its association with Scott, along with that of Rob Roy, continues to draw tourists from all over the world.

Not only famed for its beauty and its historical associations Loch Katrine also took on another important role in the mid-19th century when it became the principle drinking water source for the growing city of Glasgow. Before this, Glaswegians had to rely on contaminated

Below *The birthplace of Rob Roy MacGregor and the setting for Sir Walter Scott's* The Lady of the Lake, *Loch Katrine has been a popular destination for tourists since the early 19th century.*

water from the River Clyde and wells for their domestic water supply, cholera was rife and, in 1848, the city authorities were given responsibility for clean water and sewage disposal. Engineered by James Watt and Thomas Telford two 26-mile aqueducts were built to carry water from the loch to water treatment works at Milngavie, north of Glasgow. Construction started in 1855 and its completion in 1859 was marked on 14 October that year by an opening ceremony performed by Queen Victoria.

Despite its popularity, Loch Katrine's natural beauty and solitude have been safeguarded from the worst excesses of mass tourism by its limited road access. Visitors to the loch today can leave their cars either at the main pier complex at the eastern end (reached along the A821 from Aberfoyle or Callander) or at Stronachlachar Pier at the western end (reached via the winding B829 also from Aberfoyle). In Victorian times visitors were transported from the railway station at Aberfoyle by coach and horses to the eastern end of the loch before embarking on a pleasure cruise.

Pleasure craft have reigned supreme on Loch Katrine since the early 19th century. The first such vessel, named *Water Witch* and manned by eight strong local lads wearing kilts, was the main form of transport until 1843 when the steam-powered paddle steamer *Gypsy* arrived on the scene. Competition between the two boats was fierce until *Gypsy* mysteriously

disappeared into the waters one night - allegedly scuttled by the redundant oarsmen from *Water Witch*. She was replaced in 1845 by another paddle steamer, the *Rob Roy*, and subsequently by a second ship with the same name.

The present screw-driven ship plying the loch is the *SS Sir Walter Scott* which was built by Denny's of Dumbarton in 1899. Her maiden voyage to land-locked Loch Katrine was in itself a major feat, first being transported in pieces by barge up Loch Lomond to Inversnaid before being pulled overland by a team of horses to Stronachlachar where it was reassembled. The ship is powered by a 3-cylinder triple expansion engine and has two locomotive-type boilers which were fired by coke until 2007 when they were converted to run on bio-fuel. For more details of sailings on *Sir Walter Scott*

between April and October contact Trossachs Pier, Loch Katrine, By Callander, Stirling FK17 8HZ.
Tel. +44 (0)1877 332000
Website: www.lochkatrine.com

MYTHS AND LEGENDS

Located on the south shore near the eastern end of the loch, a small cave in Coire na Uruisgean is reputed to have been a hiding place for 17th century cattle rustlers and the traditional meeting place for Scotland's goblins. It was in this cave that Ellen Douglas, heroine of Scott's *Lady of the Lake*, hid with her father from Roderick Dhu, the outlawed chief of the Clan Alpine.

The disappearance of the paddle steamer *Gypsy* in 1844 has always

Left and below *Built in 1899 by Denny's of Dumbarton the graceful* Sir Walter Scott *has been carrying visitors across Loch Katrine for 110 years. Recently converted to run on bio-fuel, the ship operates from the Trossachs Pier complex to Stronachlachar between April and October.*

remained a mystery. The redundant oarsmen from the *Water Witch* were accused of taking her out one night and scuttling her in the loch. Taken to court they claimed in their defence that a supernatural water bull known to inhabit the loch had sunk the boat by holing its hull with its horns. The case was thrown out because the strong Gaelic dialect spoken by the men caused mayhem with the court's translator.

NATURAL HISTORY

Set in the Loch Lomond & The Trossachs National Park, Loch Katrine has recently become the focus of a large and intensive forest landscape restoration project. A partnership between Scottish Water and the Forestry Commission will result in

Left *The cross of St Andrews flies proudly from the bow of the* Sir Walter Scott *as it makes its leisurely way across Loch Katrine. Nearly half the original cost of the ship's construction was swallowed up by delivery charges when it was transported in pieces on a barge up Loch Lomond and then overland to Loch Katrine in 1899. It was then reassembled and has remained on the loch ever since.*

the restoration of around 5,000 acres of native broadleaved woodland habitat, rare in Scotland since the Middle Ages. Together with similar schemes at the RSPB reserve at Inversnaid to the west and the Woodland Trust's Glen Finglas estate to the east, this will result in the largest area of native woodland south of the Highlands. The replanting of this ancient woodland will also see the increase of wildlife species in the area including birds such as wood warbler, redstart, crossbill, golden eagle, grouse osprey and short-eared owl.

WALKING AND CYCLING

The shores around Loch Katrine offer unrivalled opportunities for both walkers and cyclists. Closed to motorists, the level road around the north shore from the Trossachs Pier complex to Stronachlachar makes a perfect day out when combined with a one-way crossing of the loch on the *Sir Walter Scott*. Car parking and bicycle hire is available at the eastern pier complex while there is a small car park and tea room at Stronachlachar.

CANOEING AND KAYAKING

As Loch Katrine is a public water supply users of the loch should avoid polluting the water. The easiest and safest access point is from Stronachlachar as the eastern end at the pier complex is usually busy with the comings and goings of the *Sir Walter Scott*. Canoeists should aviod this ship as it is slow to manoevre. A large water intake, two miles east of Stronachlachar, should also be avoided. For more information visit: www.canoescotland.com

ANGLING AND BOAT HIRE

Loch Katrine is fabled for its clear water and the amazing variety in colouration of its wild brown trout. Angling on the loch is by boat only, accessed from the western end at Stronachlachar. Permits are available from Scottish Water. Tel. +44 (0)1877 376316

TOURIST INFORMATION AND ACCOMMODATION

Trossachs Discovery Centre, Main Street, Aberfoyle FK8 3UQ. Tel. +44 (0)8452 255121. Website: www.visitscotland.com

Above *Most visitors start their journey across Loch Katrine from the Trossachs Pier complex at the eastern end, reached along the A821 from Aberfoyle. Here there is a pay car park, information centre, cafe, bar, restaurant and cycle hire facilities.*

Below *Stronachlachar with its pier and former hotel lies two miles short of the western end of Loch Katrine. Despite falling within the Loch Lomond & The Trossachs National Park the skyline here is sadly disfigured by a line of electricity pylons.*

LOCH LUBNAIG

LOCH LUBNAIG
VITAL STATISTICS
Max. length: 3.5mi
Surface area: 1.08mi^2
Average depth: 82ft
Max. depth: 146ft
Water volume: 15
billion gallons

ORDNANCE
SURVEY 1: 50,000
LANDRANGER MAP
No. 57

One of the smaller lochs in the Loch Lomond & The Trossachs National Park, Loch Lubnaig is shaped like a boomerang – its Gaelic name means crooked. Set in wooded Strathyre the loch is popular with walkers and cyclists using the former railway trackbed along its western shoreline.

HISTORY

For centuries the winding valley of Strathyre has been an important route used by people travelling between the Highlands and the Lowlands of Scotland. First used by cattle drovers on their way to market, Strathyre was later penetrated by one of General Wade's military roads built in the 18th century to ease the passage of Government troops on their way to garrisons further north.

Right *Away from the busy A87 the six-mile path, part of National Cycle Network Route 7, along the western shore of Loch Lubnaig, offers peace and tranquility although it can be busy with walkers and cyclists at weekends.*

The coming of the Callander & Oban Railway in the late 19th century transformed Strathyre, making it a popular destination for Victorian tourists. Although nominally independent the railway was financially backed and operated by the Caledonian Railway. Opened throughout in 1880, the building of the line through Strathyre and up Glen Ogle to Crianlarich and Oban took 15 years to complete. Sadly, the line as far as Crianlarich was listed for closure in the infamous 'Beeching Report' of 1963 and its demise in 1965 is still greatly mourned in the area. Fortunately the trackbed of the railway alongside Loch Lubnaig and beyond has more recently been converted into a footpath and cycleway (see WALKING AND CYCLING).

NATURAL HISTORY

Strathyre Forest falls within the Queen Elizabeth Forest Park, home to a wide range of animal and plant life. The marshes at the shallow northern end of Loch Lubnaig have been designated a Site of Special Scientific Interest.

WALKING AND CYCLING

The trackbed of the closed Callander & Oban Railway along the western shore of Loch Lubnaig now forms part of the 79-mile Rob Roy Way between Drymen, north of Dumbarton, and Pitlochry. The path also forms part of National Cycle Network Route 7 as it makes its way up from Callander, through the Pass of Leny and on up Glen Ogle to Killin. The six-mile level trackbed of the railway alongside the loch between the small car park at the Pass of Leny and Strathyre is popular with walkers and cyclists at weekends. There is ample car parking in Strathyre.

To the south of Loch Lubnaig the Pass

Below *Overlooked by Ardnandave Hill (2,345ft), the several beaches along the eastern shore of Loch Lubnaig are a popular spot for launching boats, fishing and picnics. The western shore beneath the hill can only be accessed on foot or by bike along the former railway trackbed between the Falls of Leny and the village of Strathyre.*

Left *Opened throughout in 1880, the Callander & Oban Railway transformed Strathyre into a popular destination for Victorian and Edwardian tourists. The train journey through the Pass of Leny, along Loch Lubnaig and up through Glen Ogle must have rated as one of the most scenic in the UK. Listed for closure in the 'Beeching Report' the line finally closed on 27 September 1965. Today the trackbed forms part of the Rob Roy Way long distance path and National Cycle Network Route 7.*

Below *Overlooked by Benvane (2,693ft) the shallow northern end of Loch Lubnaig has been designated a Site of Special Scientific Interest for its important marshland habitat.*

of Leny and the dramatic Falls of Leny form part of Strathyre Forest which itself is part of the Queen Elizabeth Forest Park and is managed by the Forestry Commission. From the car park at the Pass of Leny there is a footpath up to a viewpoint in Leny Wood.

The nearest Munro is Ben Vorlich (3,227ft) to the northeast of the loch but this is usually accessed from Loch Earn. Much closer to Loch Lubnaig is Ben Ledi (2,883ft) which can be climbed via a steep footpath from the Falls of Leny car park to the south of the loch.

CANOEING AND KAYAKING

Access to the loch is from the two car parks alongside the A87 at the southern end of the loch. The beaches here are also popular spots for camping.

ANGLING AND BOAT HIRE

Fishing for brown trout, char and salmon is by bank or boat. Salmon from the Forth river system run through the loch making it particularly popular with salmon anglers.

The season is from 15 March to 6 October. For permits and key to slipway contact Baynes Tackle Shop in Callander Tel. +44 (0)1877 330218

TOURIST INFORMATION AND ACCOMMODATION

Callander Tourist Information Centre, 10 Ancaster Square, Callander, Perthshire FK17 8ED. Tel. +44 (0) 8452 255121 Website: www.visitscotland.com **or** www.incallander.co.uk

**LOCH EARN
VITAL STATISTICS**
Max. length: 6.3mi
Surface area: 4mi²
Average depth: 196ft
Max. depth: 285ft
Water volume: 136
billion gallons
**ORDNANCE SURVEY
1: 50,000
LANDRANGER MAP
No. 51**

LOCH EARN

Below *Loch Earn, popular with water skiers and anglers, is also famous for an unusual tidal phenomenon known as a seiche. This is caused by pressure from the prevailing westerly winds funnelling down the steep-sided loch and setting up an oscillation of the water. The imperceptible tide created takes about 16 hours to complete each cycle.*

Geologists believe that during the last Ice Age, which began around two million years ago and ended around 11,500 years ago, an ice sheet nearly one mile thick spread outwards from the Rannoch Moor area, slowly flowing south and east. During this period the hills, mountains and glens that we know today were shaped by the scouring mechanism of this ice - Loch Earn, lying on a west-east axis in a U-shaped valley, was formed in this way. The loch also lies on a seismic fault line - a seismic station at Comrie to the east regularly records minor earth tremors in the region.

Today, Loch Earn is fed by numerous tumbling burns that flow down from the surrounding steep-sided hills and mountains - most of these are at the western end and include the Ample, Kendrum, Ogle and Beich. At its eastern end the loch's waters outflow via the River Earn to the Firth of Tay.

Unseen by visitors to the village of St Fillans, a hydro-electricity power station, part of the Breadalbane Hydro-Electric Power Scheme completed in 1961, harnesses the power of water that is carried through a tunnel from the Loch Lednock reservoir to the north.

Loch Earn is famous for a tidal phenomenon known as a seiche caused by pressure from the prevailing westerly winds funnelling down the steep-sided loch. This pressure sets up an oscillation of the water and creates an imperceptible tide which, in Loch Earn's case, takes about 16 hours to complete.

HISTORY

Artefacts from the Early Stone Age found at Lochearnhead show that the area around Loch Earn has been inhabited for many thousands of years. Crannogs, or artificial islands, dating from the Iron Age are also found at three locations around the loch. In fact the loch is steeped in history – in Scottish Gaelic its name of Loch Eireann is thought to mean 'Loch of Ireland' which dates back to the 4th century AD when the Irish Gaels were spreading eastwards into Pictish territory, bringing with them their language and culture. That the Picts stayed in the area there is no doubt – the remains of a Pictish fort at Dundurn near the eastern end of the loch dates from around the 7th century AD.

It was around this time that Christianity was introduced to the region by the early missionaries from Ireland and Iona. St Fillan, the 19th century village at the eastern end of Loch Earn, is probably named after Faolan or St Fillan of Munster who came to Scotland as a

hermit in 717AD. He is credited with preaching to the heathen Picts from Dundurn Hill and, according to folklore, possessed incredible supernatural powers including healing the sick and the mentally ill. Even his left arm was supposed to be luminious enabling him to read in the dark! The remains of an early Christian chapel probably dating from this period can be seen today, close to St Fillans golf course.

Reminders of Loch Earn's turbulent clan history are everywhere. At the eastern end is Neish Island where a 13th century castle once stood on a crannog as a stronghold for the chief of the Neishes (a tribe of the MacGregors). The Neishes were all but wiped out in 1612 when their island stronghold was attacked by rival Macnabs from Killin who had hauled their boat overland from Loch Tay. There is no trace of the castle today.

At the western end stands Edinample Castle which was built by 'Black' Duncan Campbell of Glenorchy on land once owned by the MacGregors before their

demise in the early 14th century. Completed in 1584, the castle is supposed to be haunted by its builder who was murdered by Duncan to avoid payment for his services!

To the east, halfway along Loch Earn's southern shore, is Ardvorlich House, home to the Stewarts of Ardvorlich from 1580, while on the north shore opposite lies Earnknowe, the burial ground for the McLarens of Ardveich.

Following the Jacobite rebellions of the 18th century much of Scotland's wild Highland interior was tamed by the building of military roads under the watchful eye of General Wade. One such road, completed in 1750 and linking the military garrisons of Stirling and Fort William, passed the western end of Loch Earn on its route up Glen Ogle.

The natural beauty of Loch Earn has long been a magnet for tourists and holidaymakers escaping the hustle and bustle of the big cities. As early as 1817 the pretty village of St Fillans (previously known as

Meikleport) was developed by Drummond Estates into a linear lochside resort, but it was the coming of the railways in the late 19th and early 20th centuries that transformed Loch Earn into a major tourist attraction.

At the western end of the loch the Callander & Oban Railway had opened in 1870 as far as Killin. Lochearnhead station, later renamed Balquhidder, was two miles from the village it served but in 1905 a new line was opened from Comrie along the north shore of the loch to Lochearnhead and the newly renamed Balquhidder station. Sadly, this scenic line fell victim to competition from road transport and closed in 1951. The Callander & Oban Railway route up Glen Ogle also closed in 1965.

Today Loch Earn is just as popular as a tourist destination – 50% of Scotland's population live just over an hour's drive away – but the siting of an enormous mobile home park on its southern shore near St Fillans can only be regretted.

NATURAL HISTORY
Loch Earn is one of 22 lochs in the Loch Lomond & The Trossachs National Park. Established in 2002, the National Park is home to a wide range of habitats – mountains, woods rivers and lochs – and wildlife species including otter, water vole, capercaillie, black grouse, osprey, red squirrel and red deer.

WALKING AND CYCLING
While the minor road that passes through woodland along the southern shore of the loch is relatively quiet and popular with anglers, the highlight for walkers and cyclists can be accessed at Lochearnhead. Here

the former Callander & Oban Railway trackbed is now a well-surfaced footpath and cycleway (National Cycle Network Route 7) which runs through Rob Roy country from Callander, through the Pass of Leny, alongside Loch Lubnaig and up Glen Ogle to Killin. For Munro lovers the pyramid-shaped peak of Ben Vorlich (3,230ft) is reached via a path from Ardvorlich on Loch Earn's south shore.

WATER SPORTS
Loch Earn is famous for its water sports activities including water skiing, canoeing and sailing. For more details contact Lochearnhead Water Sports Centre (Tel. +44 (0)1567 830321 or visit: www.lochearnhead-water-sports.co.uk) For dinghy and keelboat sailing contact Loch Earn Sailing Club (Tel +44 (0)1764 685229 or visit: www.lochearnsc.com)

ANGLING AND BOAT HIRE
Loch Earn is a popular destination for anglers and is well known for its healthy population of large brown trout. Fishing from the bank or from a boat close to the shore should bring good results. For fishing permits and boat hire contact Drummond Estates
Tel. +44 (0)1567 830400
Website: www.drummondtroutfarm.co.uk

TOURIST INFORMATION AND ACCOMMODATION
Callander Tourist Information Centre, 10 Ancaster Square, Callander FK17 8ED
Tel +44 (0)8452 255121
Website: www.visitscotland.com

Left Popular with anglers, the wooded south shore of Loch Earn is accessed by a minor road from St Fillans. Located by the lochside near this tranquil spot at Coillemhor is a memorial stone which marks the temporary place of internment of the body of Major James Stewart of Ardvorlich who died c.1660. The body was later moved to the Stewart family vault at Dundurn.

LOCH LEVEN

**LOCH LEVEN
VITAL STATISTICS**
Max. length: 3.4mi
Surface area: 5.6mi²
Average depth: 11.5ft
Max. depth: 65ft
Water volume: 11
billion gallons

ORDNANCE
SURVEY 1: 50,000
LANDRANGER MAP
NO. 58

Below *Overlooking Castle Island and Lochleven Castle near Kinross, Kirkgate Graveyard was once the site of a Chapel of Ease built by the monks of St Serf's Island. The graveyard contains many interesting gravestones including that of Robert Burns Begg, solicitor and grand nephew of Robert Burns the poet.*

The largest body of freshwater in lowland Britain, Loch Leven has shrunk in size since it was partially drained by the canalisation of the River Leven in the early 19th century. Over 1,000 acres of additional farmland were thus created around the loch at a time when agricultural land was in much demand. Water levels are controlled by sluices on the four-mile man-made cut that flows westward from the southern end of the loch. Needless to say the loch is now very shallow with only two 65ft-deep 'kettle holes' that were formed by melting glacier ice over 10,000 years ago.

Loch Leven has two major islands, St Serf's and Castle, both of them much larger since the lowering of the water level nearly 200 years ago.

Not only steeped in history, Loch Leven is also one of the most important wildfowl nature reserves in Europe.

HISTORY

Evidence of human occupation around Loch Leven can be found close to the A911 at the north end of the loch. Here, marking the site of an ancient burial ground, the two Orwell standing stones are estimated to date back about 4,300 years. In the loch, Castle Island was originally the site of a 5th century Pictish fort - the present Lochleven Castle on the island dates back to the 14th century.

Early Celtic Christian's arrived in the region around the 6th century AD and established a community of Culdee monks on St Serf's Island. A monastery was later built here and became an important centre of learning - in the 15th century the Prior of St Serfs, Andrew Wynton, wrote the first history book about Scotland, *Orygynal Cronykil*. The monastery was demolished in the 19th century but the remains of a chapel have survived. As the island is now an important breeding ground for waterfowl and gulls there is no public access.

Meanwhile, Lochleven Castle had been built at the beginning of the 14th century by English soldiers of Edward I. Within a very short time it had been seized by William Wallace and, by the late 14th century, had been granted to William Douglas, 1st Earl of Douglas. It was here that Mary, Queen of Scots was imprisoned in 1567 and forced to abdicate in favour of her young son, James. A year later she managed to escape from the castle with the help of her gaoler's family. The castle changed hands in 1675 when it was sold to Sir William Bruce who went on to build Kinross House on the western shore of the loch and by the end of the century Lochleven Castle had become an uninhabited ruin. It is now in the care of Historic Scotland and can be visited between April and September via a small ferry that runs from the pier at Kinross.

Set on the west shore of the loch, Sir William Bruce's Kinross House was completed in 1693 and is considered to be one of the finest late 17th century buildings in Scotland. Although the house is closed to the public the formal gardens are open from April to September.

The canalisation of the River Leven and subsequent lowering of the loch's water levels in the early 19th century not only increased the amount of valuable agricultural land available to the Kinross Estate but also provided water power for new local industries - as a result, by 1830, local people found employment in linen flax mills, corn mills, whisky stills, snuff mills, paper mills and textile bleaching.

Railways first came to Kinross in 1860 when a joint station was opened by the Kinross-shire Railway and the Fife & Kinross Railway. Platforms were also built alongside Loch Leven for use when curling events were held on the frozen loch. Curler's Platform, as it was known, closed in 1921. The railway through Kinross closed in 1970.

NATURAL HISTORY

The most important breeding ground for ducks in Europe, Loch Leven is a National Nature Reserve, a Site of Special Scientific Interest and a Special Protection Area. The loch is home to tufted duck, mallard, gadwall, shelduck, pochard and shoveler while during the winter months it is also visited by tens of thousands of other wildfowl from Europe and Scandinavia making it a site of global importance – nearly the entire world population (about 25,000) of Icelandic pink-footed goose are resident here in the winter.

The draining of the loch in the early 19th century led to an increase in the

Below *Loch Leven has long been an important centre for angling, wildfowling and curling. The Kinross Curling Association was founded in 1688 and during extremely cold winters huge curling tournaments or 'bonspiels' were held on the frozen lake.*

surrounding wetlands which now support orchids, dragonflies and wading birds such lapwing, snipe, curlew and redshank. Loch Leven Nature Reserve is managed by Scottish Natural Heritage while the Vane Farm Nature Reserve at the southern end is run by the RSPB. Here, there is a car park, visitor centre, café and trail to the top of Vane Hill. For more details: Tel. +44 (0) 1577 862355 or visit: www.rspb.org.uk

WALKING AND CYCLING

Suitable for walkers and cyclists, the 7½-mile Loch Leven Heritage Trail runs from the Pier at Kinross around the north and east shores of the loch to the RSPB Vane Farm Nature Reserve. A car park and picnic site at Findatie allows access to the southern end of the Trail. For more information visit: www.lochlevenheritagetrail.co.uk

For cyclists, Route 1 of the National Cycle Network passes through Kinross.

CANOEING AND KAYAKING

Although banned until 2004, canoes and kayaks are now allowed on the loch. There is no public access to St Serf's Island.

ANGLING AND BOAT HIRE

Loch Leven is famous for its wild brown trout which are used to stock fisheries worldwide. There is no bank fishing – fishing is 'fly only' and must be from boats that can be hired from Loch Leven Fisheries at their pier at Kinross. Here there is also an Angling Centre with angling tuition courses and facilities for disabled anglers. For more details: Tel. +44 (0) 1577 865386 or visit: www.lochlevenfisheries.co.uk

TOURIST INFORMATION AND ACCOMMODATION

Heart of Scotland Visitor Centre, Junction 6, M90, Kinross KY13 7NQ Tel. +44 (0) 1577 863680 Website: www.perthshire.co.uk

Left *Set on Castle Island in Loch Leven, Lochleven Castle dates back to the early 14th century when it was used as a state prison. The most famous prisoner held here was Mary, Queen of Scots who was incarcerated from 1567 until her escape a year later. It was here that she abdicated in favour of her young son, James, who later went on to become James I of England and Scotland. Managed by Historic Scotland, the castle can be reached via a summer-season ferry from Kinross Pier.*

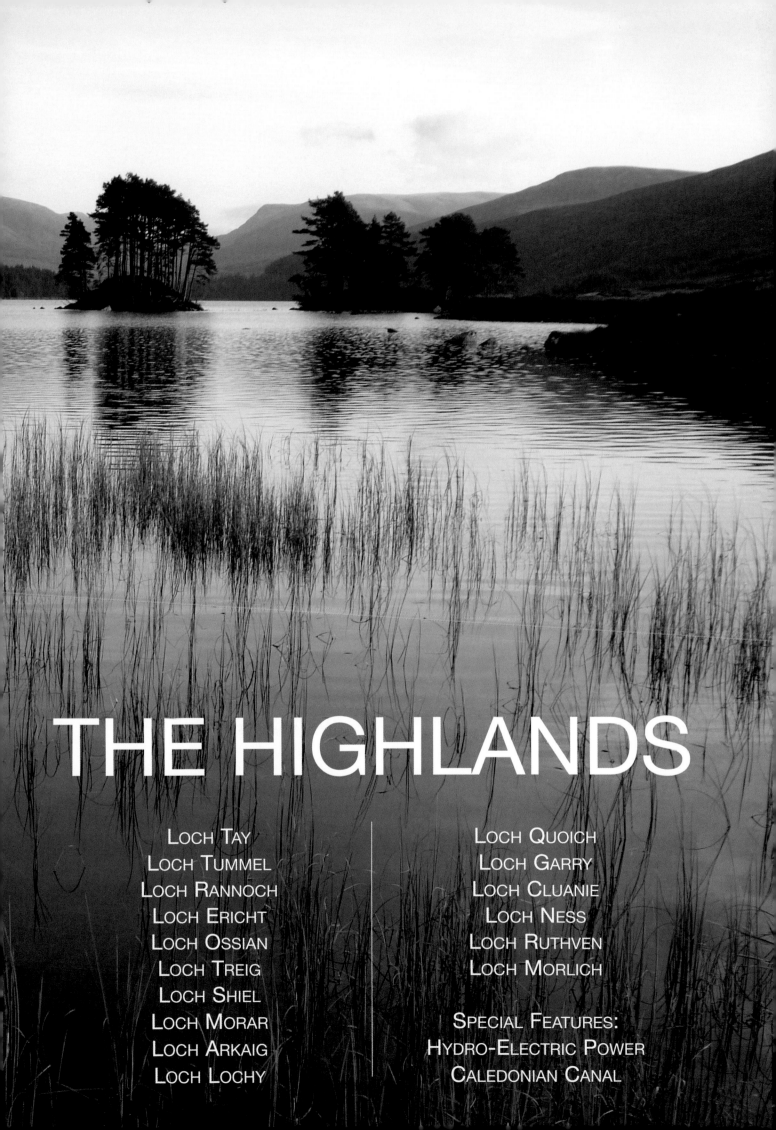

THE HIGHLANDS

LOCH TAY

The sixth largest loch in Scotland by area, Loch Tay lies on the Loch Tay Fault, a geological fault line that cuts across the metamorphic rocks which lie southeast of the Great Glen. The bend in the middle of the loch was created by later glacial erosion along the line of the fault. To the north of the loch is Ben Lawers, which at 3,984ft is the eleventh highest mountain in Britain.

Loch Tay forms part of the vast Breadalbane hydro-electric power scheme which, with its seven power stations, became operational in 1961 and involved the contruction of dams and tunnels linking several lochs in the area.

HISTORY

Until the notorious Highland Clearances of the late 18th and early 19th centuries, the fertile soils on the lower slopes of Ben Lawers supported many farming communities. Evidence of human activity around Loch Tay dates back to before the Bronze Age – stone circles, standing stones and 'cup and ring' marked rocks all point to the area being settled for at least the last 5,000 years.

Probably an ancient sacred site, a yew tree at Fortinghall in Glen Lyon, to the north of Loch Tay, is reckoned to be 3,000 years old making it the oldest yew in the world. The remains of Iron Age crannogs, or artificial islands, can also be seen at either end of the loch. Open to visitors from April to October, the Scottish Crannog Centre has recreated a crannog at Kenmore. For more information visit www.crannog.co.uk

Dating from Medieval times, the remains of numerous shielings, or temporary summer residences for farmers grazing their flocks, can still be found around the 1,600–2,000ft contours on the lower slopes of Ben Lawers. By the 16th century much of the land around Loch Tay was owned by the powerful Clan Campbell. Taymouth Castle, one mile northeast of Kenmore, stands on the site of Balloch Castle which was built in 1550 for Sir Colin Campbell of Glenorchy. The current neo-Gothic pile (not open to the public) was built by the Campbells of Breadalbane in the early 19th century when family fortunes were in the ascendancy.

At the opposite end of the social scale and the opposite end of the loch lies Moirlanich Longhouse, near Killin, a superb example of a traditional cruck frame cottage and byre dating from the mid-19th century. The house is owned by the National Trust of Scotland and is open from May to September.

By the end of the 18th century there were around 3,500 people living around Loch Tay. Most of them were crofters scratching a living from the land but their future was bleak - the year 1834 saw thousands of them evicted from their

LOCH TAY
VITAL STATISTICS
Max. length: 14mi
Surface area: 10.2mi²
Average depth: 213ft
Max. depth: 492ft
Water volume: 377 billion gallons
ORDNANCE SURVEY
1: 50,000
LANDRANGER MAP
NO. 51

homes by the 2nd Marquis of Breadalbane to make way for modern sheep farming. Whole communities disappeared for ever from around the loch, forced to sail across the Atlantic to a new life in Canada. These 'clearances' were so thorough that by 1850 the population around Loch Tay had dropped to only 100. Today the deserted village of Lawers, with the ruins of the church, laird's house, dwellings, mill, and barns, is a stark reminder of those dark days.

The coming of the railway to Killin and Loch Tay in 1886 transformed the loch into a major tourist attraction. Promoted by the Earl of Breadalbane the railway joined the Callander & Oban Railway at remote Killin Junction station. By the end of the 19th century, visitors were able to travel by train from Glasgow to Killin, cruise and take lunch on *The Lady of the Lake* paddle steamer before being taken by charabanc to Aberfeldy station for their return trip to Glasgow. The railway to Loch Tay closed in 1939 and the steamer service in 1949.

MYTHS AND LEGENDS

According to local legend the Lady of Lawers was a 17th century prophetess who uttered sayings in Gaelic. Some of her prophecies concerned social changes in the area, no doubt now understood to refer to the 'clearances', while others foretold the future of the Breadalbane family. Her existence, however, has never been proved.

NATURAL HISTORY

The afforested slopes of Drummond Hill above Kenmore at the northern end of Loch Tay form part of the Forestry Commission's Tay Forest Park. It is thought to be the site of Scotland's first managed forest which was planted by Black Duncan, the Earl of Breadalbane, in the early 17th century. Drummond Hill was also one of the first purchases of land for the Forestry Commission after World War I. The endangered capercaillie is being re-introduced into the upper parts of this pine forest while more common sights are red squirrel, pine

marten and red deer. Osprey are known to nest along the shore line nearby.

Dominating Loch Tay is Ben Lawers (3,981ft), Perthshire's highest mountain, which lies to the north of the loch. Owned by the National Trust ofr Scotland this National Nature Reserve covers nearly 12,000 acres on the southern slopes of the mountain and the adjacent Tarmachan range and is regarded by botanists as one of the most important areas for rare alpine plants, such as saxifrage, alpine forget-me-knot and roseroot, anywhere in the UK. The

Below *The sixth largest loch in Scotland by area, Loch Tay has been a popular destination for Scotland's city-dwellers for over 100 years. Outdoor pursuits in and around the loch include a wide range of watersports, fishing, walking, mountain biking and Munro climbing.*

Below *The remains of several Iron Age crannogs, or artificial islands, can be seen around Loch Tay's shoreline. The Crannog Centre near Kenmore features a reconstructed crannog built by the Scottish Trust for Underwater Archaeology and is open to the public from April to October.*

reserve also supports many species of breeding birds including ring ouzel, red grouse, ptarmigan, curlew and raven. Other rare species include the wildcat and viviparous lizard.

WALKING AND CYCLING

The many forest trails in the Tay Forest Park can be reached from the Forestry Commission car park near Mains of Taymouth. For Munro baggers various paths lead to the summit of Ben Lawers and the Tarmachan range from the car park south of the Lochan na Lairige dam.

This is reached along the minor road that leads from the A827 six miles east of Killin. The Falls of Acharn and Hermit's Cave can be reached on foot from Acharn village two miles west of Kenmore, via the minor road that skirts the loch's south shore. National Cycle Network Route 7 also runs along this road between Killin and Kenmore.

WATERSPORTS

Three centres around the loch provide tuition and hire facilities for a wide range of watersports:

Croft-Na-Caber Watersports & Activity Centre Tel. +44 (0)1887 830588

Loch Tay Highland Lodges
Tel. +44 (0)1567 820051

Loch Tay Boating Centre
Tel. +44 (0)1887 830291

ANGLING AND BOAT HIRE

Loch Tay is famous for its salmon, brown trout, pike and charr and fishing is from bank and boat. The western end of the loch is run by the Killin & Breadalbane Angling Club (Tel. +44 (0)1567 820833) while the eastern end towards Kenmore is run by the East Loch Tay Angling Club (Tel. +44 (0)1887 830526). Permits can be obtained

from various hotels in Killin, Loch Tay Highland Lodges at Milton Morenish, Ben Lawers Hotel in Lawers, Kenmore Post Office, Kenmore Caravan Site and the Ben Lawers Hotel. Boat hire is also available from many of the above.

TOURIST INFORMATION AND ACCOMMODATION

Aberfeldy Tourist Information Centre, The Square Aberfeldy, Perthshire PH15 2DD. Tel. +44 (0)1887 820276
Website:
www.perthshire.co.uk

LOCH TUMMEL

LOCH TUMMEL VITAL STATISTICS

Max. length: 6.8mi
Surface area: 3mi²
Average depth: 60ft
Max. depth: 130ft
Water volume: 31 billion gallons

ORDNANCE SURVEY 1: 50,000 LANDRANGER MAPS NOS. 42/52

Although much smaller than many other Highland lochs, tranquil Loch Tummel exudes its own unique charm. The loch forms part of a major hydro-electric scheme, although its main claim to fame is the famous vantage point of 'Queen's View' located at its eastern end.

HISTORY

Today the afforested slopes high above the northern shore of the loch form Allean Forest, itself part of the Tay Forest Park. However, thousands of years ago, this area was inhabited by our early ancestors who left behind the stone circle, standing stones, burial cairns and hillforts that can be seen today. The area is also littered with ruined farmsteads, a reminder of those dark days of the 'Clearances' during the late 18th/early 19th centuries. Various waymarked trails in Allean Forest take in several of these archaeological sites (see WALKING, AND CYCLING).

The first half of the 18th century was a tumultuous time in Scotland. Following the 1715 Jacobite Rebellion the British government was determined to control the Highlands and sent General George Wade to oversee the construction of a series of military roads linking garrisons in the region. One of these roads, completed in 1730, passes through Tummel Bridge at the

Above *The view along Loch Tummel towards Schiehallion (3,552ft) from 'Queen's View' is one of the most famous in Scotland. This lofty viewpoint can be reached on foot from a nearby Forestry Commission car park and visitor centre.*

Below *Allean Forest, with its waymarked walking and mountain bike trails, rises up from Loch Tummel's northern shore. Ardgualich Farm caravan park and campsite (Tel + 44 (0) 1796 472825) is located right on the water's edge.*

western end of the loch. The B846 to Aberfeldy still follows the original route of this road.

Loch Tummel's main claim to fame is the famous viewpoint known as 'Queen's View' set high above the loch at its northeastern end. Although visited by Queen Victoria in 1866, the viewpoint is possibly named after 'Queen' Isabella, the first wife of Robert the Bruce, although she never actually became Queen of Scotland due to her untimely death in 1296. Mary, Queen of Scots may also have visited this spot but whichever queen it is named after the view along the loch to the distant peak of Schiehallion is certainly one of the most famous in Scotland. 'Queens View' can be reached on foot from the Forestry Commission car park and visitor centre.

Constructed in the early 1930s, the Tummel hydro-electric scheme links lochs Ericht, Rannoch and Tummel. There are nine power stations located along this 'cascade' including one at Tummel Bridge in the west and at Pitlochry in the east.

NATURAL HISTORY

Set within the Tay Forest Park, Loch Tummel and Allean Forest to the north are designated a National Scenic Area. The forest, planted with Douglas fir, pine, spruce and larch, is home to a wide range of seed-eating birds, including siskin crossbill and the tiny goldcrest. While red squirrel and roe deer are more common sights, the nocturnal wildcat is more elusive. To the east, with its 34 separate pools, the fish ladder at Pitlochry Dam is a great place to see salmon as they swim up the River Tummel to spawn.

WALKING AND CYCLING

There are several waymarked mountain bike and walking trails through Allean Forest. Starting point for these is the Forestry Commission car park on the B8019 along the north shore of the loch. Several of the trails take in archaeological sites including the remains of an 8th century fort and a partly restored 18th century farmstead.

While the busy and narrow B8019 to the north of the loch is not an ideal cycling route, the minor road along the south shore is relatively quiet and affords stopping off points for a lochside picnic.

CANOEING, KAYAKING AND SAILING

Access is best from the minor road along the south shore of the loch where there are several sheltered beaches. Stopping off points include an island at the eastern end and sandy beaches along the northern shoreline. The Loch Tummel Sailing Club is located towards the western end on the south shore. For more details visit: www.lochtummelsc.org

ANGLING

Trout fishing is by any method, but from bank only although a few areas are restricted. Permits are available at various outlets in Pitlochry.

TOURIST INFORMATION AND ACCOMMODATION

Pitlochry Tourist Information Centre, 22 Atholl Road, Pitlochry PH16 5BX Tel. +44 (0) 1796 472215 Website: www.perthshire.co.uk

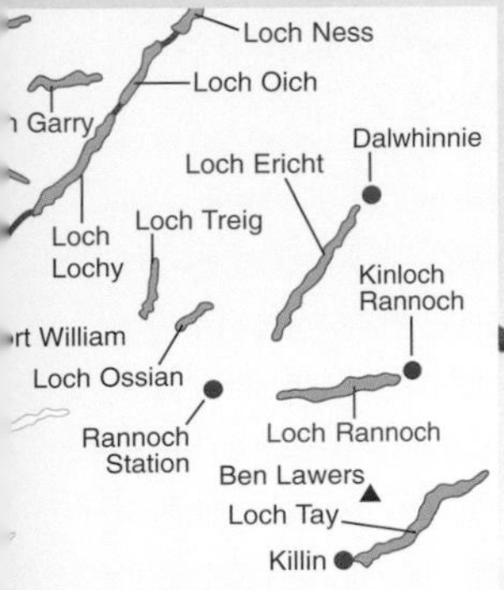

LOCH RANNOCH

Loch Ness
Loch Oich
Garry
Dalwhinnie
Loch Ericht
Loch Treig
Loch
Lochy
Kinloch
Rannoch
rt William
Loch Ossian
Rannoch
Station
Loch Rannoch
Ben Lawers ▲
Loch Tay
Killin

LOCH RANNOCH
VITAL STATISTICS
Max. length: 9.3mi
Surface area: 7.4mi²
Average depth: 131ft
Max. depth: 393ft
Water volume: 168
billion gallons

ORDNANCE
SURVEY 1: 50,000
LANDRANGER MAPS
NOS. 42/51

Scoured and shaped by glaciers during the last Ice Age (two million – 11,500 years ago), the area around Loch Rannoch contains many fascinating glacial features including examples of roche moutonee and kame deposits just beyond the eastern end of the loch overlooking Dunalastair Water. 600 million-year-old limestone pavements are also found to the north and south of here while the peak of Schiehallion (3,552ft) to the southeast consists mainly of extremely hard quartzite, formed from sand by extreme heat and pressure. The mountain was also the scene of a famous experiment in 1774 when the Astronomer Royal, Rev Neville Maskelyne, correctly calculated the weight of the Earth.

To the west the boggy wilderness of Rannoch Moor was once part of the Caledonian Forest that covered much of northern Scotland following the end of the last Ice Age.

Loch Rannoch is fed by waters from Rannoch Moor via Loch Laidon and Loch Eigheach in the west and outflows via the River Tummel to Loch Tummel in the east.

HISTORY

Stone axes found on the slopes of Schiehallion show that humans have lived around Loch Rannoch for over 5,000 years. Settlement and cultivation

Below *Famous for its population of large ferox trout, Loch Rannoch is a popular venue for anglers. In the distance the quartz-topped peak of Schiehallion, owned by the John Muir Trust since 1999, is a favourite climb for Munro lovers.*

began around 1500BC while the heathen Picts who lived here from the first millennium were visited by early missionaries from Iona such as St Blane, who went on to convert them to Christianity from the 6th century AD onwards.

During medieval times Loch Rannoch was on the 'Road to the Isles' which ran from Pilochry across Rannoch Moor to Glen Coe, Fort William and Mallaig. During this period Rannoch was a hotbed of clan feuding and cattle rustling – of the seven clans active in the area (Roberstson, Stewart, Menzie, MacGregor, MacDougall, MacDonald and Cameron) the MacGregors were the most feared. Their lawlessness was severely dealt with by Government troops in the 18th century. Visitors to the loch today can follow a 'Clan Trail' which is marked by information plaques around the shoreline. At the western end of the loch, Rannoch Barracks was originally built to house Government troops under Hector Munro who were stationed here after the Jacobite Rising in 1745.

Communications in the area were vastly improved by the Government following the failed rebellion. By the end of the 18th century roads and bridges had been built and Kinloch Rannoch, at the eastern end of the loch, had been established as a retirement village for soldiers. This wasn't a successful social experiment so local people were given the right to own their own land.

By the 1860s the Highlands were being opened up to visitors by the building of railways. However, the nearest station was at Pitlochry, some 13 miles to the east of Loch Rannoch, on the Highland Railway's main line from Perth. The opening of the North British Railway's West Highland line between Glasgow and Fort William in 1894 transformed this remote part of Scotland. Passengers could (and still can) travel overnight from London and be deposited the next morning at lonely Rannoch station five miles to the west of the loch. The great outdoors was now easily accessible and the age of tourism had been born.

By the 20th century there were many schemes to harness the power of water in Scottish lochs to generate electricity. One of the first of these hydro-electric schemes to be built was at Loch Rannoch. Opened in 1930, the power station near Bridge of Ericht on the northwestern shore of the loch is powered by water flowing along a three-mile tunnel from Loch Ericht to the north. Other power stations and dams were built at Gaur to the west and Tummel Bridge to the east. Today there are a total of nine such power stations in the area feeding electricity into the National Grid.

NATURAL HISTORY

Once covered by the native trees of the Caledonian Forest the area around Loch Rannoch has suffered in recent centuries from extensive deforestation caused by indiscriminate felling and the subsequent planting of alien species for the commercial forestry industry.

Part of the Tay Forest Park managed by the Forestry Commission, the Black Wood of Rannoch Nature Reserve on the south shore of the loch contains some of the last remnants of the Caledonian Forest and supports a wide range of plants, insects, birds and animals such as red squirrel and pine marten. Sadly the alien mink has also inhabited the area following its escape from fur farms near Pitlochry.

The birdlife around the loch is impressive – birds of prey include golden

eagle, hen harrier, short eared owl, merlin, peregrine falcon and even the rare osprey, while the waters of the loch support many species of duck and, in winter, whooper swan and large flocks of greylag goose.

To the west of Loch Rannoch, the Rannoch Moor National Nature Reserve is the largest blanket bog in Europe.

To the southeast of the loch the mountain of Schiehallion and land to the east of its peak which has been owned since 1999 by the John Muir Trust is designated as part of a Site of Special Scientific Interest, an area of National Scenic Beauty and a Geological Conservation Review. Within its boundaries are a wide variety of upland habitats which survive on the underlying limestone. Over 60 species of upland

Below *Five miles west of Loch Rannoch is remote Rannoch station. Complete with a snug tea room, the station is served by trains on the West Highland line between Glasgow and Fort William and the 'Caledonian Sleeper' from Euston.*

Below *Located on the northwestern shore of the loch, Rannoch hydro-electric power station is powered by water carried from Loch Ericht along a 3-mile tunnel. In the foreground is an ancient crannog topped with a Victorian folly.*

birds have been recorded here with breeding species including hen harrier, merlin, black grouse, ring ouzel and the rare ptarmigan. A growing number of red deer also inhabit the south side of the mountain.

WALKING, CYCLING AND CLIMBING
The forests, hills, mountains and glens around Loch Rannoch offer walkers a wide range of terrain. In particular Rannoch Forest and the Black Wood of Rannoch, part of the Tay Forest Park, has miles of tracks and paths for walkers keen to discover the remnants of the native Caledonian Forest and the multitude of bird, animal and plant life. The nearest car park, picnic and campsite is located 2½ miles west of Kinloch Rannoch on the south shore minor road. For more information visit: www.forestry.gov.uk

and search for Tay Forest Park.

For Munro lovers the distinctive peak of Schiehallion to the south east of Loch Rannoch can be reached from a car park at Braes Foss, five miles east of Kinloch Rannoch on the Tomphubil minor road. Other Munros nearby include Carn Mairg and Meall Garbh.

With numerous opportunities for lochside picnics the fairly level and quiet 22-mile road route around the loch makes an ideal day out for cyclists

ANGLING AND BOAT HIRE
Loch Rannoch is famous for its large ferox trout (over 20lbs recorded) as well as char, pike, brown trout, salmon, perch and rainbow trout. The loch not only has good areas of shallows at its western end but also a minor road around its shore that makes bank access much easier.

LRCA permits are available from the Dunalastair Hotel in Kinloch Rannoch (www.dunalastair.co.uk). For more information on fishing and boat hire on Loch Rannoch also visit:
www.tayfishingperthshire.co.uk
www.fishingnet.com

CANOEING, KAYAKING AND SAILING
Loch Rannoch Watersports Centre at Kinloch Rannoch offers courses, instruction and hire for sailing, canoeing, kayaking (Tel. +44 (0) 1882 632242).

TOURIST INFORMATION AND ACCOMMODATION
Pitlochry Tourist Information Centre, 22 Atholl Road, Pitlochry, Perthshire PH16 5BX
Tel. +44 (0) 1796 472215/472751
Website: www.perthshire.co.uk

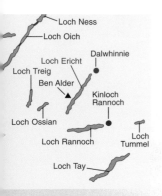

Loch Ness
Loch Oich
Dalwhinnie
Loch Ericht
Loch Treig
Ben Alder
Kinloch
Rannoch
Loch Ossian
Loch Rannoch
Loch Tummel
Loch Tay

LOCH ERICHT
VITAL STATISTICS
Max. length: 14.3mi
Surface area: 7.18mi²
Average depth: 199ft
Max. depth: 511ft
Water volume: 248
billion gallons

ORDNANCE
SURVEY 1: 50,000
LANDRANGER MAP
NOS. 42

LOCH ERICHT

The tenth largest freshwater loch in Scotland, Loch Ericht is a narrow and long finger of water lying on a northeast-southwest axis that is, uniquely, dammed at both ends. Surrounded by mountains and Munros, of which the highest and nearest are Ben Alder (3,765ft) and Beinn Bheoil (3,342ft), the loch is inaccessible by road apart from a private gated entrance near Dalwhinnie.

The loch is fed at its northern end by an aqueduct that carries water from remote Loch Cuaich. The low-lying dam at this end of the loch protects the village of Dalwhinnie from flooding. At its dammed southern end, water outflow is controlled along a three-mile tunnel to a hydro-electric power station on the north shore of Loch Rannoch (see pages 70-73) or via the River Ericht.

In recent years, Loch Ericht's remoteness, inaccessibility and total lack of commercial development have made it a favourite destination for walkers, climbers and anglers.

HISTORY

Situated north of the strategically important Pass of Drumochtar, the small village of Dalwhinnie at the northern end of the loch dates back to the late 17th century when an inn was established here on the important cattle drovers' road between the Highlands and the lowland market at Crieff.

Communications through Dalwhinnie were much improved in 1725 when General George Wade built the junction of two of his military roads here. These were constructed to link forts in this remote Highland region and enable Government troops to quickly suppress further rebellion in Scotland after the Jacobite Rebellion of 1715. However, during the later 1745 Rebellion, Wade was left with egg on his face as the Jacobite forces made a speedy advance into England. He was dismissed for his failure to halt the Scots.

The coming of the railway through Dalwhinnie in the 19th century transformed the Highlands. Opened in 1863, the Highland Railway's main line between Perth and Inverness made the region easily accessible to Victorian travellers for the first time. Large sporting estates and lodges were established around Loch Ericht, attracting well-heeled city punters for a weekend of excellent shooting and fishing.

To add to this *joie de vivre*, the Dalwhinnie Distillery was opened in 1897. The highest distillery in Scotland, it stands close to the banks of the

Above *Dalwhinnie, the jumping off point for Loch Ericht, is served by trains between Glasgow/Edinburgh, Perth and Inverness. It is but a short walk from Dalwhinnie station to the shores of this unspoilt loch.*

Below *Much of the land around the shores of Loch Ericht is owned by the Loch Ericht Estate and borders onto the BBC's Monarch of the Glen's 'Glenbogle Estate'. The Loch Ericht Estate rents out luxury self-catering accommodation at three locations along the loch's shoreline - Camusericht, Corrievarkie and An Tochailt Lodges. For more information visit: www.lochericht.co.uk*

River Truim, a tributary of the famous River Spey.

Loch Ericht formed part of one of Scotland's first hydro-electricity generation schemes in 1930 when its northern and southern ends were dammed. Acting as a giant reservoir for a power station on the north shore of Loch Rannoch, Loch Ericht is fed by water from Loch Cuaich via an aqueduct.

NATURAL HISTORY

The remote lower mountainsides around Loch Ericht once supported great tracts of the ancient Caledonian pinewoods – their names live on today, marked on the OS map as the Ben Alder, Dalnaspaidal, Talla Beith and Rannoch Forests. While tracts of commercial coniferous woodland are found along the loch's western shore there are still pockets of native deciduous trees to be found on the opposite shore. Wildlife, ranging from red deer, red squirrel, pine marten and mountain hare to golden eagle and the rare osprey, is plentiful in this wilderness.

WALKING, CLIMBING AND CYCLING

No roads encircle Loch Ericht making it an ideal destination for walkers wishing to savour some of the best scenery in the Highlands. Foot or mountain bike access to the fairly level track that runs along the western shore of the loch is at two locations: (a) at the north end – via a level crossing gate near Dalwhinnie station or under the railway viaduct to the south; and (b) at the south end – via a forestry track from Bridge of Ericht on the north shore of Loch Rannoch. Five miles along the track from Dalwhinnie lies Ben Alder bothy (allegedly haunted by a ghost of a ghillie who hanged himself there) and from here a track leads to Loch Pattack, Culra bothy and Ben Alder or, eventually, to Kinloch Laggan.

Route 7 of the National Cycle Network runs through Dalwhinnie.

ANGLING

Fishing for brown trout on Loch Ericht is by way of bank only. There is no vehicular access to the loch. For further information and permits contact Loch Ericht Hotel, Dalwhinnie, Highlands PH19 1AG (Tel. +44 (0) 1528 522257).

CANOEING AND KAYAKING

Access is at the northern end but with difficulty (see WALKING, CLIMBING AND CYCLING). Paddling down this long loch against strong headwinds can be hard work.

TOURIST INFORMATION AND ACCOMMODATION

Kingussie Tourist Information Centre Highland Folk Museum, Kingussie, Highland PH21 1JG. Tel: 0845 2255121 Website: www.visithighlands.com

LOCH OSSIAN
VITAL STATISTICS
Max. length: 3mi
Surface area: 1.35mi²
Average depth: 65ft
Max. depth: 131ft
Water volume: 15
billion gallons

ORDNANCE
SURVEY 1: 50,000
LANDRANGER MAPS
NOS. 41/42

LOCH OSSIAN

Ringed by hills and mountains, remote Loch Ossian is set in the 52,000 acres of wilderness that make up the Corrour Estate on the northeastern edge of Rannoch Moor. Fed by waters from the surrounding mountains this small loch outflows northwards along the River Ossian via Loch Ghuilbinn to the River Spean at Moy.

Apart from a long and winding private forestry road from the A86 in Glen Spean there is no road access to this peaceful and magical place. However, those wishing to visit the loch take the only mode of transport available: by train to Corrour station on the scenic West Highland Line. Featuring in Danny Boyle's film *Trainspotting* starring Ewan McGregor, Corrour station, one mile to the west of the loch, is served by trains, including the Caledonian Sleeper from London, from Fort William and Glasgow. From the station there is a track down to the western end of the loch where there is a state-of-the-art eco Youth Hostel.

Visitors to the newly opened Corrour Lodge at the eastern end of the loch are met at the station by a four-wheel-drive vehicle.

HISTORY

For centuries remote Loch Ossian could only be accessed via the 'Road to the Isles' cattle drovers' road that cut across Rannoch Moor from Skye to the markets in central Scotland. This all changed in 1891 when Sir John Stirling-Maxwell (1866–1956) of Pollok, Glasgow, bought the Corrour Estate which includes Loch Ossian. The eldest son of Sir William Stirling-Maxwell, John succeeded his father to the baronetcy in 1878 at the age of 12. In later years he was to become a Conservative MP, served as Chairman of the Forestry Commission in its early years and was a founder member of the National Trust of Scotland.

Wanting to build a new lodge at the eastern end of Loch Ossian, Sir John also actively encouraged the building of the West Highland Railway between Glasgow and Fort William. Opened in 1894 across the peat bogs of Rannoch Moor the line transformed access to the Corrour Estate with the opening of Corrour station. The railway not only brought the much-needed building material needed for the lodge but also a small steam boat, the *Cailleach*, which was

Below *Reached only by train to Corrour Station on the West Highland Line, Loch Ossian nestles between mountains in the 52,000-acre wilderness of the Corrour Estate. This magical place is the perfect destination for those wishing to 'get away from it all'. Accommodation is available at the lochside eco-Youth Hostel, at Corrour Lodge and at Corrour Station House.*

brought in pieces to Corrour and then resassembled on the loch. The boat was first used to transport building material for the lodge which was completed in 1899. Until 1910, when a road around the south shore of the loch was built, visitors to the estate were carried from the station by pony and trap to the boat house on Loch Ossian and then taken on a short cruise to the lodge at the eastern end. With his keen interest in plants and trees, Sir John laid out the rhododendron gardens that can still be seen at Corrour Lodge today. The hostel for hillwalkers, built in the old boathouse at the western

end of the loch, was opened in 1931. Today, this Youth Hostel is one of the most remote and eco-friendly in Britain.

The idyllic pattern of life on this gentleman's estate continued until 1942 when Corrour Lodge burned down; only its chapel, game larder and school house remained. In 1995 the Corrour Estate came under new ownership and is now run by the Corrour Trust who are adopting a holistic approach to protecting the land and moving towards a new balance between sporting estate and natural wilderness. Designed by US architect Moshe Safdie, a new lodge with

Above *The 'Caledonian Sleeper' arrives at Corrour Station after its long overnight journey from London Euston. Leaving the mayhem of London behind the night before, visitors to Loch Ossian can awake refreshed at this remote spot which features in Danny Boyle's famous film,* Trainspotting.

self-catering accommodation, was completed in 2003.

NATURAL HISTORY
The Corrour Estate's 52,000 acres of wilderness is home to an enormous range of plant and wildlife. Mammals

Left and below *Originally opened in 1931 in the old boathouse at the western end of the loch, remote Loch Ossian Youth Hostel now boasts many environmentally-friendly features including wind and solar power, grey water and dry toilet systems.*

seen on the estate include red deer – by far the most numerous and managed since 1834 – roe deer, sika deer, pine marten, badger, otter and mountain hare. Birds include golden eagle, ptarmigan, red and black grouse, golden plover, black throated diver, peregrine falcon, merlin, goshawk and dotterel.

WALKING AND CYCLING

This is hill walking country at its best – the loch's remote location, lack of roads and numerous Munros (there are 20 on the Corrour Estate) make it a favourite destination for those wishing to 'get away from it all'. The area is also an excellent and safe location for mountain biking. For details of organised walks and mountain bike hire contact the Corrour Estate. Tel. +44 (0) 1397 732200 Website: www.corrour.co.uk

BOAT RENTAL

Canoes, rowing boats and motorboats can also be hired from the Corrour Estate. They are fully equipped with safety gear and operational instructions are given beforehand.

ANGLING

With its peace and solitude Loch Ossian must rate as one of the most beautiful inland fishing locations in Scotland. Containing wild brown trout and large pike the loch is suitable for wet fly or dapping or from a boat hired from the Corrour Estate. Fishing permits are available through the estate office.

TOURIST INFORMATION AND ACCOMMODATION

Rail services to Corrour Station:
Website: www.scotrail.co.uk
Loch Ossian Youth Hostel:
Scottish Youth Hostel Association
Tel. +44 (0) 845 293 7373
Website: www.syha.org.uk
Self-catering accommodation at Corrour Lodge:
Tel +44 (0) 1397 732200
Website: www.corrour.co.uk)
Corrour Station House (restaurant and B&B):
Tel. +44 (0) 1397 732236
Website: www.corrourstationhouse.co.uk
General Tourist Information:
Fort William Tourist Information Centre,
15 High Street, Fort William PH33 6DH
Tel. +44 (0) 845 2255121
Website: www.visithighlands.com

LOCH TREIG

**LOCH TREIG
VITAL STATISTICS**
Max. length: 5.4mi
Surface area: 2.7mi²
Average depth: 196ft
Max. depth: 492ft
Water volume: 92
billion gallons

ORDNANCE
SURVEY 1: 50,000
LANDRANGER MAP
NO. 41

Below *The construction of the Lochaber hydro-electric scheme in the 1920s and 1930s raised the water levels of Loch Treig by around 36ft. Opened in 1894 the West Highland Railway, seen here on the opposite bank, also had to be realigned at a higher level above the loch. The best way to see Loch Treig is to travel along this spectacular railway between Fort William and Corrour - from the latter station a 3-mile boggy track leads to the southern end of the loch.*

Formed by the erosive action of glaciers during the last Ice Age, Loch Treig grew much larger and deeper some 70 years ago when it became a reservoir for the Lochaber hydro-electric scheme. Then, the building of a dam at its northern end raised water levels considerably, submerging the two small communities of Kinlochtreig and Creaguaineach at its southern end.

Features of glacial erosion by meltwater, unique in Scotland, were discovered in the loch during a period of low water level in 1996. The meltwater forms found at that time include scallops, chutes, chute pools and potholes - features which would have have been formed above the water table.

HISTORY
Today, Loch Treig is inaccessible by road apart from at its northern end at Fersit which is reached via a lane off the A86.

Before the building of the reservoir in the 1930s the two communities at its southern end had historically been important markets at the end of cattle drove roads. Apart from Creaguaineach Lodge perched on the southern shore they now lie submerged beneath the waters of the loch.

Opened in 1894, the West Highland Railway between Glasgow and Fort William was built along the eastern shore of the loch. The railway is still open today and is considered to be one of the most spectacular rail journeys in the world. The raising of the water levels during the building of the Lochaber hydro-electric scheme in the 1930s led to a realignment of the railway at a higher level alongside the loch.

The building of the Lochaber hydro-electric scheme was a massive civil engineering project that took around 16 years to complete. Built by Balfour, Beatty to generate electricity for a new aluminium factory at Fort William, the work involved the damming of Loch Treig and nearby Loch Laggan and the

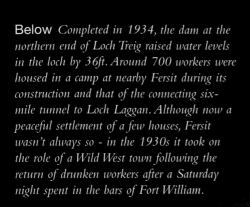

Below *Completed in 1934, the dam at the
northern end of Loch Treig raised water levels
in the loch by 36ft. Around 700 workers were
housed in a camp at nearby Fersit during its
construction and that of the connecting six-
mile tunnel to Loch Laggan. Although now a
peaceful settlement of a few houses, Fersit
wasn't always so - in the 1930s it took on
the role of a Wild West town following the
return of drunken workers after a Saturday
night spent in the bars of Fort William.*

blasting, through solid rock, of a 15-mile tunnel designed to carry 860 million gallons of water each day. Water levels in Loch Treig are kept topped up by water fed through a six-mile tunnel from Loch Laggan. A 21-mile narrow gauge railway was also built between Fort William and Loch Treig to assist Balfour, Beatty during the construction period and afterwards for maintenance purposes. This remote and inaccessible line, known as the Upper Works Railway, finally closed in 1976 but its trackbed can still be traced across the hillsides from Fort William and around the intake valve shafts at the northern end of the loch.

MYTHS AND LEGENDS

According to legend the Scottish Highlands, particularly the area around Loch Treig, is frequented by a crone goddess known as the Cailleach. She is easy to spot as she is dressed in grey, carries a stick and has long white hair and a blue face with one eye in the middle of her forehead! Apart from her ghostly apparition she is also the protector of wild deer and for this she has been respected by local hunters for centuries.

NATURAL HISTORY

The remote and inaccessible steep sided hills and mountains around the loch are favourite haunts of golden eagle and red deer. Red squirrel and pine marten can also be spotted in the woodland and forest at the north end of the loch.

WALKING AND CYCLING

The area around Loch Treig is a paradise for serious walkers and mountain bikers.

The south end of the loch can be reached along a three-mile track from Corrour station, served by trains on the West Highland line. From Creaguaineach Lodge tracks lead across remote terrain to Kinlochleven in the southwest, Glen Nevis in the west and up Lairig Leacach to the mountain pass between the peaks of Sgurr Innse and Ston Coire and on to Spean Bridge. Bothies for overnight stays can be found at Staoineag, Loch Chiarain and in Lairig Leadach. Suitable footwear, clothing, maps, compass and provisions are an absolute necessity in this remote and wild region.

For less strenuous exercise the track from the car park at Fersit, at the north end of the loch, to the Treig Dam and on to the valve shafts on the northwestern shore offers stunning scenery and a chance for a leisurely picnic.

Four Munros overlook the loch: to the west are Stob a Choire Mheadhoin (3,329ft) and Stob Coire Easain (3,657ft); to the east are Stob Coire Sgriodain (3,211ft) and Meall Garbh (3,201ft).

CANOEING AND KAYAKING

Access at the north end of the loch is difficult as vehicles are barred from the road down from the car park at Fersit. Access at the southern end is also difficult - via the boggy three-mile trail from Corrour station.

ANGLING

Free fishing for wild brown trout and pike although there are no boats or launching facilities. The best fishing is at the southern end which can be accessed on foot along a three-mile boggy track from Corrour railway station.

TOURIST INFORMATION AND ACCOMMODATION

Fort William Tourist Information Centre, 15 High Street, Fort William PH33 6DH Tel. +44 (0) 845 2255121 Website: www.visithighlands.com

Left and above *The valve shafts on the northwestern shore of Loch Treig control the water flowing down the 15-mile tunnel to the aluminium works at Fort William. Blasted through solid rock and lined with concrete the 15ft diameter tunnel is large enough for a single-decker bus to drive through.*

HYDRO-ELECTRIC POWER

Hydro-electricity is electricity generated by the gravitational force of flowing or falling water and is the most widely used renewable energy source in the world. Requiring vast amounts of dammed water held in reservoirs it is not surprising, given the high amounts of rainfall, large catchment areas and the location of so many deep freshwater lochs, that Scotland has 85% of the UK's hydro-electric energy resource.

One of the first uses of domestic hydro-electricity in Scotland was that installed by Lancashire millionaire George Bullough in Kinloch Castle on the island of Rum at the end of the 19th century. However, this was but a small scheme compared to other projects.

The production of aluminium requires vast amounts of cheap electricity and it was to the Highlands that the British Aluminium Company looked for the site

Below *Built as part of a hydro-electric scheme for an aluminium smelter in Fort William in the 1930s, the dam at the northern end of Loch Treig raised water levels by 36ft.*

of their first factory in the late 19th century. This was built at Foyers on the east shore of Loch Ness in 1896 but, soon, demand outstripped supply and a new factory was built at Kinlochleven in 1904. Following World War I the demand for aluminium steadily grew and the British Aluminium Company eventually built another smelter at Fort William. Hydro-electricity for this plant was, and still is, generated by 860 million gallons of water flowing along a 14-mile tunnel each day from Loch Treig. The loch's water levels were raised by 36ft by the building of a dam at its northern end and a further reservoir was also built by the damming of nearby Loch Laggan. Completed by Balfour, Beatty in 1943 the Lochaber hydro-electric scheme was one of the largest civil engineering projects ever undertaken in Britain.

In addition to hydro-elecricity generation for aluminium production there are now a large number of such schemes operating throughout Scotland that supply electricity to the National Grid. The first of these was built in the

1930s for the Grampian Electricity Supply Company - dams were built at either end of Loch Ericht and water fed through a tunnel to a power station on the north shore of Loch Rannoch. This scheme was soon enlarged to include power stations at Loch Tummel and at Pitlochry.

Founded in 1943 the North of Scotland Hydro-Electric Board was the prime mover behind many other schemes that were built in the Highlands after World War II. The damming of existing lochs and the building of tunnels, aqueducts and power stations reached its peak in the 1950s. The following is a list of the larger schemes and the lochs and lochans involved:

Loch Sloy 1950-1959
Loch Sloy, Lochan Shira Mor, Lochan Sron Mor
Tummel-Garry 1930-1958
Loch Ericht, Loch Rannoch, Loch Tummel, Loch Seilich, Loch Cuaich, Loch Faskally, Loch Errochty
Conon Valley 1957-1961
Loch Fannich, Loch Luichart, Loch Glascarnoch, Loch Vaich, Loch Achanalt,

Loch Meig, Loch Achonachie
Affric-Cannich 1952
Loch Mullardoch, Loch Benevean
Strathfarrar-Kilmorack 1963
Loch Monar, Loch Beannachran
Moriston-Garry 1957
Loch Quoich, Loch Garry, Loch Loyne,
Loch Cluanie
Loch Shin 1960
Breadalbane 1961
Lochan na Lairige, Loch Tay, Loch
Breaclaich, Loch Lednock, Loch Earn,
Loch Lyon, Loch Giorra
Awe/Ben Cruachan 1965
Loch Nant, Loch Awe
Foyers 1975
Loch Mhor, Loch Ness

The Ben Cruachan scheme generates
electricity using pumped storage – during
times of off-peak electricity, water from
Loch Awe is pumped by reversible
turbines up to a dammed reservoir in the
mountain above; at times of peak demand
the water is released to the generators
located deep down inside the mountain.

Below *Built in 1930 for the Grampian Electricity Supply Company, the power staton at Loch Rannoch is powered by water flowing through a three-mile tunnel from Loch Ericht.*

Above *Built as part of the Moriston-Garry hydro-electric scheme in 1957, the dam at the eastern end of Loch Quoich is the largest rockfill dam in Scotland. Water flows down a tunnel from the 125ft-high dam to a power station on the River Garry.. The raising of water levels in the loch submerged a road, crofters' cottages and the 19th century Glenquoich Lodge.*

**LOCH SHIEL
VITAL STATISTICS**
Max. length: 16.7mi
Surface area: 7.6mi²
Average depth: 132ft
Max. depth: 393ft
Water volume: 174
billion gallons

ORDNANCE
SURVEY 1: 50,000
LANDRANGER MAP
NO. 40

LOCH SHIEL

Formed by glacial erosion during the last Ice Age, Loch Shiel is a narrow, steep-sided ribbon of water that outflows to the sea at its southern end via the short River Shiel. Just a few feet above current sea levels, the loch was once a sea loch until falling sea levels thousands of years ago left it landlocked. While the majority of its shoreline is wooded, this gives way to shallow marshland and a fertile plain in the south. For centuries virtually undisturbed by human activity, the loch and its diverse habitats are now an important area for wildlife and nature conservation.

HISTORY

Steeped in history, the area around Loch Shiel has been occupied since Neolithic times – the low-lying fertile land at its southern end and easy access to the harvest of the sea encouraging early farming settlements. Preaching Christianity to the native Picts, early

missionaries first visited Loch Shiel in the 6th century AD and built a chapel on the island now known as Eilean Fhianain. Named after St Finan, a teacher of St Columba, the ruined chapel and adjoining burial ground can be seen today in the narrowest part of the loch just over one mile east of Dalelia.

Linked to the sea by the once navigable River Shiel, Loch Shiel provided an important communications artery through the mountains to its northern end. By the 10th century AD the area was being visited by Viking raiders, some of whom remained to occupy the fertile area around Acharacle. Their presence was not welcomed by the indigenous people and in 1140 they were driven away by an army led by the famous Celtic-Norse Chief, Somerled. The village of Acharacle at the southern end of loch is the site of the defeat of the Danish Chief, Torquil, by Somerled. His victory paved the way for centuries of rule over much of northwest Scotland and the Hebrides by the

MacDonalds of Clan Ranald, led by the Lord of the Isles. Castle Tioram, at the mouth of the River Shiel, later became their stronghold.

The MacDonalds became strong supporters of the Stewart Kings of Scotland and were involved in attempts to regain the throne of Britain for the exiled King James. During the Jacobite Rebellion of 1745, Bonnie Prince Charlie was secretly landed by the French navy in the nearby Sound of Arisaig. A few days later he was rowed up Loch Shiel to Glenfinnan for the gathering of his army before marching south into England. The rest of this story is well known with the eventual defeat of the

Jacobites at the Battle of Culloden in 1746. The monument at Glenfinnan was erected in 1815 to mark the place where Bonnie Prince Charlie raised his standard in 1745.

Glenfinnan, at the northern end of the loch, is also the site of another famous structure. The 21-arch curving concrete viaduct that carries the railway from Fort William to Mallaig was completed in 1901. Designed by Robert McAlpine, or 'Concrete Bob' as he was affectionately known, the viaduct is famous the world over having featured in numerous films, including the Harry Potter series, and on Scottish banknotes. Loch Shiel is also the location of the fictional

Below *With the famous monument marking the spot where Bonnie Prince Charlie raised his standard in 1745, the 21-arch concrete curving railway viaduct that features in Harry Potter films, railway museum and Loch Shiel boat cruises, Glenfinnan is a popular destination with visitors. Suitable for walkers and mountain bikers, a 13-mile forestry track leads along the south shore of the loch to Polloch.*

Hogwarts Lake in the 'Harry Potter' films.

The coming of the railway to Glenfinnan in 1901 led to a regular mail steamer service down the loch to Acharacle Pier. The North British Railway's timetable of 1922 shows one return service each weekday, the journey taking 2½ hours including a stop at Dalelia. Sadly this service ceased in the 1960s.

MYTHS AND LEGENDS

Loch Shiel is apparently inhabited by a fast-moving 70ft-long monster with three humps known as Shielagh. Sightings go back to 1874 with many being documented by a local Benedictine priest, Father Cyril Dieckhoff. The most recent sighting was in 1998 but, as with the rest of Scotland's loch monsters, one has never been caught, dead or alive.

NATURAL HISTORY

Mainly untouched by human activity and with a wide diversity of habitats, Loch Shiel and its shoreline is one of the most important areas in the Highlands for wildlife and nature conservation. Its importance is reflected in numerous designations such as Sites of Special Scientific Interest, Special Areas of Conservation, National Nature Reserves, Special Protection Area and a Biosphere Reserve. High above the loch, the surrounding mountainsides and peaks are home to golden eagle, raven and large herds of red deer.

The marshland of Claisha Moss at its southern end supports numerous species of dragonfly, specialised bog plants, hen harrier and white-fronted goose. The deciduous woodlands on the northern shore of the loch include stands of native oak, birch, ash, hazel and alder. Rich in moss and fern they support a wide variety of wildlife including pine marten, red squirrel and wildcat. Loch Shiel is also visited by numerous breeding water birds including the black-throated diver while otter are a regular sight in and around its waters. One of the only remaining remants of native pinewood in the west of Scotland can be seen near Glenfinnan on the northern slopes of Meall na h-Airigh.

WALKING AND CYCLING

From Dalelia at the southern end of Loch Shiel, a lochside track leads to a memorial and a pier opposite St Finan's Island. The steep coastline north of here is only accessible by boat. A 13-mile forestry track suitable for walkers and mountain bikers stretches down the south shore from Glenfinnan to Polloch. There is road access at either end. There are also numerous trails around Glenfinnan, accessed from the National Trust of Scotland car park.

CANOEING AND KAYAKING

Loch Shiel's peace and tranquility make it a popular destination for canoeists and kayakers. Access at the southern end is from the old steamer pier at Ardshealach, while at the northern end access is from the pier at Glenfinnan.

ANGLING AND BOAT HIRE

Sadly, sea trout for which the loch was once famous are now in decline. At the southern end of the loch, permits and boat fishing for brown trout and salmon can be arranged through Dalelia Farm (Tel. +44 (0) 1967 431253) or Loch Shiel Hotel (Tel. +44 (0) 1967 431224 or visit: www.lochshielhotel.com)

BOAT TRIPS

Highland Cruises operate guided wildlife and historic scenic cruises along Loch Shiel from the pier at Glenfinnan. For more details Tel. +44 (0) 1687 470322 or visit: www.highlandcruises.co.uk

TOURIST INFORMATION AND ACCOMMODATION

Fort William Tourist Information Centre, 15 High Street, Fort William PH33 6DH Tel. +44 (0) 845 2255121 Website: www.visithighlands.com

Below *Former London & North Eastern Railway Class 'K1' 2-6-0 No. 62005* Lord of the Isles *passes slowly over Glenfinnan Viaduct with the summer-only 'Jacobite' train from Fort William to Mallaig.*

LOCH MORAR

**LOCH MORAR
VITAL STATISTICS**
Max. length: 11.8mi
Surface area: 10.3mi²
Average depth: 284ft
Max. depth: 1,016ft
Water volume: 507
billion gallons

**ORDNANCE
SURVEY 1: 50,000
LANDRANGER MAP
NO. 40**

Below *The only way to explore Loch Morar and its many wooded islands is by boat. The Loch Morar Boat Hire Company in Morar will hire out rowing boats or small outboards. Fishing permits and permits to launch motorised boats are available from the Loch Superintendent (see text for details).*

Formed by glacial erosion during the last Ice Age (2 million years – 11,500 years ago), steep-sided Loch Morar is the fifth largest loch in Scotland and also the deepest freshwater body in the British Isles – it is also the 17th deepest in the world. Surprisingly Loch Morar's catchment area is much smaller than other similarly sized Scottish lochs – less than 10% than that of Loch Ness. Loch Morar has eight wooded islands, the majority located at the western end of which Eilean a Phidhir is the largest.

The loch's proximity to the sea at its western end – only half a mile at the narrowest point – indicates that it was once a sea loch millions of years ago. With a surface altitude of around 33ft the loch outflows to the sea via waterfalls on the short River Morar. On the coast low tide reveals the famous Silver Sands of Morar, a major attraction for visitors during the summer. The sands are also famous as one of the locations used in the filming of 'Local Hero' starring Burt Lancaster.

HISTORY
The western end of Loch Morar is famous as the site of the Battle of Morar which was fought in 1602 between Clan

MacDonell of Glengarry on one side and Clan Mackenzie and Clan Ross on the other. The battle followed years of bitter feuding in which the Mackenzies pillaged the MacDonell's lands around Morar and led to much bloodshed on both sides. Its outcome, however, was considered a strategic victory for the Mackenzies who were subsequently given the disputed lands.

Following the Jacobite Rebellion of 1745 and the defeat at the Battle of Culloden the following year the aged and scheming Chief of Clan Fraser, Simon Fraser, hid from Government forces in a hollow tree on one of Loch Morar's small wooded islands. His hiding place was revealed and, after a trial in London in 1747, the unfortunate man became the last person to be executed by beheading in Britain.

Apart from the village of Morar and a few small hamlets at the western end of the loch, the rest of Loch Morar's long shoreline is uninhabited and inaccessible in most places apart from by boat. This

Above *Tourism, fish farming and sheep raising are the mainstay of the local economy. Sheep farming was only introduced to the area during the notorious Highland Clearances at the end of the 18th and early 19th centuries.*

was not always so but the infamous Highland Clearances of the late 18th and early 19th centuries saw most of the local crofters driven out of their homes by absent landlords to make way for sheep farming. All of the settlements on the north shore to the east of Bracorina, at Kinlochmorar at the eastern end and all of those on the southern shore are now deserted. Only one or two holiday homes are lived in for a few months of the year.

The opening of the Mallaig Extension

of the West Highland Railway from Fort William in 1901 failed to halt the depopulation of the area around Loch Morar although it did boost Mallaig's fishing industry. Fish farming, sheep raising and tourism (including the summer-only 'Jacobite' steam train) are now the mainstay of the local economy.

MYTHS AND LEGENDS
Some say that in Loch Morar there is a competitor to the famous Loch Ness

Monster. Known as Morag, the brown serpent-like creature, 20–30ft long, has been seen on numerous occasions since the 19th century. Many of the sightings were witnessed by more than one person with the most dramatic occurring in 1969 when a speedboat and its two occupants were attacked by a long brown creature with three humps. When fired upon the creature sank from sight. Legend also has it that an underground tunnel links Loch Morar with Loch Ness and that Morag and the Loch Ness Monster are the same creature.

NATURAL HISTORY
Loch Morar was once famous for its salmon and sea trout runs but, sadly, their

Below *Today, Loch Morar's remoteness and inaccessibility attract those wishing to escape the rat race. These qualities also attracted the secretive Special Operations Executive during World War II when they set up training schools at Meoble Lodge, to the south of the loch, and at Swordland Lodge on the north shore.*

numbers have reduced due to biological pollution from salmon farms. Birdwatchers will need to have a good pair of legs when exploring around the loch as much of it is only accessible on foot or by boat (see BOAT HIRE below).

WALKING AND CYCLING
A circular route from the village of Morar along the north shore of the loch also involves a passenger ferry and a railway journey. From the end of the minor road at Bracorina a path leads along the north shore passing Brinacorry Island and Swordland Lodge to South Tarbet Bay, a distance of four miles. From here a ½-mile track leads north to Tarbet Bay where a connection can be made

with the ferry to Mallaig via Loch Nevis. For ferry times and fares:
Tel. +44 (0)1687 462320
Website: www.knoydart-ferry.co.uk
To complete the circle a train can be caught from Mallaig back to Morar.

CANOEING AND KAYAKING
Exploring the many wooded islands at the western end of Loch Morar is best achieved from a canoe or kayak. A launch permit is not required on the loch for canoes, windsurfers, float tubes or any boat without an engine that can be launched without a trailer.

For more information contact the Loch Superintendent:
Tel. +44 (0)1687 462388

ANGLING AND BOAT HIRE
Fishing on Loch Morar is mainly brown trout with the occasional salmon and sea trout. Fishing is permitted from the bank and from boats. For permits contact the Loch Superintendent (see left). For boat hire contact Loch Morar Boat Hire (Tel +44 (0)1687 462520). Guided fishing tours on the loch are also available (Tel. +44 (0)1397 712476).

TOURIST INFORMATION AND ACCOMMODATION
Mallaig Tourist Information Centre, The Pier, Mallaig PH41 4SQ
Tel. 0845 2255121
website: www.visithighlands.com

LOCH ARKAIG

LOCH ARKAIG
VITAL STATISTICS
Max. length: 11.8mi
Surface area: 6.9mi²
Average depth: 131ft
Max. depth: 298ft
Water volume: 156
billion gallons

ORDNANCE
SURVEY 1: 50,000
LANDRANGER MAPS
NOS. 33/34/40

Loch Arkaig lies to the west of the Great Glen Fault which was formed over 360 million years ago during major volcanic activity in the region. However, the Highland scenery that we know today was shaped during the last Ice Age which began around two million years ago. Ending around 11,500 years ago, the Ice Age glaciers scoured and moulded the glens and mountains into the breathtaking scenery that makes Scotland so unique. When the glaciers melted, the deep glens filled with water – in this way Loch Arkaig was formed. With a surface elevation of 141ft above sea level and fed by numerous tributaries such as the Pean and Dessarry, the waters of the loch outflow at the eastern end into Loch Lochy via the River Arkaig.

HISTORY

From the late 13th century ownership of the lands around Loch Arkaig had been bitterly disputed by two clans – the Mackintoshes and the Camerons. The land had originally been owned by the Clan Chattan who were united with Clan Mackintosh in 1291 when Eva, the daughter of the former clan's chief, married Angus, the chief of the latter clan. Through this marriage the two clans became united as the Chattan Confederation. However, within a few years the lands around the loch were seized by Clan Cameron, provoking over 350 years of bitter feuding between the two clans. Many battles were fought over ownership of the land including the Battle of Drumlui which took place around 1335. In this instance, the Camerons were defeated but the bloodshed carried on for centuries even though the Mackintosh claim was upheld by both the Lord of the Isles and King David II.

The vexed question of ownership was eventually solved in 1665 when 1,500 Mackintosh men faced 1,200 Cameron men at the Fords of Arkaig at the eastern end of the loch. The stand-off lasted a week but sense finally prevailed when the Camerons agreed to buy the land from their rivals.

Eilean Loch Airceig is a small island at the eastern end of the loch is the site of a ruined chapel and the former burial ground of the Camerons of Lochiel. Today the ancestral home of Lochiel, Chief of the Clan Cameron, at nearby Achnacarry, now houses the clan museum which is open to the public.

During the late 18th and early 19th centuries the Highlands and islands of Scotland witnessed the forced displacement of the rural population during a period of agricultural change. People living on the land around Loch Arkaig did not escape these 'clearances', as they became known. Today a stone cairn, erected in 2002 under a rowan tree on the lochside at Murlaggan, stands as a fitting memorial to members of the Macmillan family from Loch Arkaig who sailed in 1802 to start a new life in Upper Canada.

MYTHS AND LEGENDS

Many Scottish lochs have stories of mysterious creatures lurking in their depths and Loch Arkaig is no exception. According to James Harris, 3rd Earl of Malmesbury, who was a foreign minister during the Victorian era, the loch is home to a water horse. This was verified in 1857 by his stalker who had

Below *Located west of the Great Glen and set amidst beautiful Highland scenery Loch Arkaig is the perfect location for walkers, cyclists, canoeists, wild campers and anglers wishing to escape the 21st century rat race.*

Left *At the eastern end of Loch Arkaig the waterfalls at Eas Chia-aig thunder with water tumbling down from mountain streams. A car park and picnic site are provided for visitors. The bridge here was a filming location for 'Rob Roy' (1995) starring Liam Neeson.*

witnessed a horse-like creature swimming in the loch on several occasions. Needless to say the 'Lake-Horse' as it became known has never been captured.

Apart from its own 'monster', Loch Arkaig is also rumoured to be the hiding place of a large consignment of Spanish gold that was brought ashore by the French at Arisaig in 1746 in support of the Jacobite Rebellion. Some say that it has never been found.

The seven cases of gold were landed a few days after the Battle of Culloden where the Jacobites were defeated by a

Below *A long and winding road closely hugs the north shore of Loch Arkaig to it western extremity. With virtually no traffic the route offers perfect conditions for cyclists amidst fantastic Highland scenery.*

combined Hanoverian army. Much of the gold, intended to assist Jacobite leaders to escape, was buried near Loch Arkaig and eventually found its way into the hands of the fugitive Macpherson of Cluny, head of Clan Macpherson who was hiding in a cave on Ben Alder. Although some of the gold found its way to Bonnie Prince Charlie not all of it was recovered and is presumed to still lie hidden somewhere around Loch Arkaig.

NATURAL HISTORY

The jewel in the crown by the shores of Loch Arkaig is the Allt Mhuic Reserve which is managed jointly by the Butterfly Conservation Society and Forestry Commission Scotland. Access to the reserve is from a car park located on the north shore road three miles from the eastern end of the loch. An area of grassland, moorland and native woodland set between two large conifer plantations, the reserve is home to 14 species of butterfly as well as moths, dragonfly, dippers, chats and flycatchers. Visitors to the reserve may also see otter, pine

marten, golden eagle, osprey and diver. In addition to the wide range of wildlife the reserve is also home to several orchid species. For more information visit: www.butterfly-conservation.org

WALKING AND CYCLING

The Eas Chia-aig forest car park at the eastern end of the loch is an ideal starting point for several walks. From here a four-mile track leads up into the steepsided and forested Gleann Cia-aig passing several spectacular waterfalls en route. The track ends at ruins known as Fedden set far below the 3,066ft peak of Sron a Choire Ghairbh. Return to the car park is via the same track.

Another excellent walk from the car park follows a Forestry Commission track through woodlands along the south shore to a bothy at the foot of Glen Mall. Distance for the return journey is 5½ miles.

The narrow road which follows the north shore of Loch Arkaig to its western extremity sees little traffic and makes an excellent scenic route for cyclists. Places to visit en route include the Allt Mhuic

Above *For serious walkers only - from the western end of Loch Arkaig tracks lead up Glens Dessary and Pean to several distant destinations. Taking the track up Glen Dessary for about five miles leads to the lower slopes of four closely grouped Munros of which Sgurr na Ciche (3,411ft) is the highest.*

Reserve and the memorial, at Murlaggan, to members of the Macmillan family who left Loch Arkaig in 1802 to start a new life in Canada.

For more serious walkers and Munro lovers the adventure starts at the western end of the loch where the road ends and there is a small car parking and turning area. From here tracks lead through stunning Scottish wilderness to Glenfinnan (9 miles), Kinlocheil (10 miles), Morar (23 miles) and Tomdoun (18 miles). Taking the track up Glen Dessary towards the head of Loch Nevis for about five miles leads to the lower slopes of four closely grouped Munros – Sgurr nan Coireachan (3,125ft), Garbh Chioch Bheag (3,175ft), Garbh Chioch Mhor (3,322ft) and Sgurr na Ciche (3,411ft). Needless to say, suitable footwear and clothing should be worn when embarking on these expeditions together with survival rations, a compass and map. The official line is that walkers are entering remote, sparsely-populated and potentially dangerous mountain country and should be adequately experienced and equipped.

CANOEING AND KAYAKING
Canoeing or kayaking combined with wild camping in the quiet secluded bays of Loch Arkaig surely must rate as a fantastic experience for lovers of Scotland's remote spots. The only drawback is the unwanted attention from midges during the summer months!

ANGLING
With its backdrop of stunning Highland scenery the wild and lonely Loch Arkaig is popular with anglers. The loch holds pike, trout, char and ferox trout and

permits are obtained from an honesty box at Bunarkaig on the B8005 where the river Arkaig enters Loch Lochy. Here there is a list of charges on the wall and you can pay by cash or cheque. Fishing off the bank usually gets good results but as there is no local boat hire anglers must make their own arrangements.

TOURIST INFORMATION AND ACCOMMODATION
Fort William Tourist Information Centre, 15 High Street, Fort William, Lochaber PH33 6DH
Tel: +44 (845) 2255121
Website: www.visithighlands.com

Left and below *People living on the land around Loch Arkaig did not escape the 'clearances' of the late 18th and early 19th centuries. Today a stone cairn, erected in 2002 under a rowan tree on the lochside at Murlaggan, stands as a fitting memorial to this terrible period when members of the Macmillan family from Loch Arkaig sailed from Fort William in 1802 to start a new life in Upper Canada.*

LOCH LOCHY

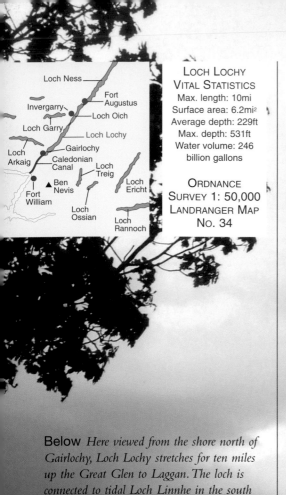

LOCH LOCHY
VITAL STATISTICS
Max. length: 10mi
Surface area: 6.2mi²
Average depth: 229ft
Max. depth: 531ft
Water volume: 246
billion gallons

ORDNANCE
SURVEY 1: 50,000
LANDRANGER MAP
NO. 34

Shaped by glacial action during the last Ice Age, Loch Lochy is the most southwesterly of the three deep freshwater lochs (the others are Loch Oich and Loch Ness) that lie in the depression known as the Great Glen Fault. Formed over 360 million years ago during major volcanic activity in the region, this large strike-slip fault separates the Northern Highlands from the Grampian Highlands.

HISTORY

Two major clashes between feuding clans have taken place around the shores of Loch Lochy. The first, on a hot summer's day in 1544, was a bloody affair that took place between Clan Cameron, under the command of Ewen Cameron, and Clan Ranald, under the command of John Moydartach, on one side and Clan Fraser under the command of the 3rd Lord Lovat on the other. They met at Kilfinnan, at the northwestern end of the loch, and the outcome of the battle is unclear depending which side you prefer to believe – either way many were killed.

Visitors to Kilfinnan graveyard today can see a stone mausoleum for the Clan MacDonnell of Glengarry.

The second clash was not so much a battle but a posturing stand-off which took place in 1665 near Achnacarry at the Fords of Arkaig. This time the Chattan Confederaton, made up of 16 clans led by Clan Mackintosh, faced the Clan Cameron in a long-running dispute over lands around nearby Loch Arkaig. After a week of stalemate the dispute was settled when the Camerons bought the lands from their adversaries. North of Gairlochy, Achnacarry Castle, the ancestral home of Lochiel, Chief of the Clan Cameron, now houses the clan museum.

Loch Lochy also forms part of the Caledonian Canal (see pages 116–117) between Inverness and Corpach, near Fort William. Linking all of the lochs in the Great Glen, the 62-mile canal with 29 locks was built by Thomas Telford and completed in 1822.

MYTHS AND LEGENDS

Lizzie, the Loch Lochy monster – a humped plesiosaur-type creature similar to that reputed to live in neighbouring Loch Ness – has apparently been seen surfacing in the loch on several occasions over the last 90 years. The first documented sighting was in 1929 when two local gamekeepers thought they saw a large creature that swam along the loch for about a mile before submerging. There have been other sightings since then and more recently a 20ft-long 'creature' was detected by sonar moving at a depth of 200ft in the loch.

Below *Here viewed from the shore north of Gairlochy, Loch Lochy stretches for ten miles up the Great Glen to Laggan. The loch is connected to tidal Loch Linnhe in the south and Loch Oich in the north via locks and the Caledonian Canal. On the far shore the busy A82 closely hugs the loch while above it in the trees are the remains of General Wade's military road and the long-closed railway from Spean Bridge to Fort Augustus.*

NATURAL HISTORY

With its wide range of habitats such as lowland fen, swampland and woodland the Great Glen is an important refuge for rare birds, butterflies, insects, trees and plants. South Laggan Fen at the northern end of Loch Lochy is a Site of Special Scientific Interest. Away from the roads, visitors to the loch shores and the surrounding hills and forests are likely to see otters, red squirrels, mountain hare, red deer and golden eagle.

WALKING AND CYCLING

The Great Glen Way, a 73-mile long distance path between Inverness and Fort William, follows the western shore of the loch. Forestry Commission car parking is available at Clunes on the B8005 two miles north of Gairlochy while there is a small car park to the north near Laggan Locks. Great Glen Way website: www.greatglenway.com

For more strenuous exercise the Loch Lochy Munroes – Sron a Choire Ghairbh and Meall na Teanga – are reached via a long and steep forest trail from Kilfinnan.

CANOEING AND KAYAKING

Loch Lochy is a popular venue for canoeists who normally follow the wooded western shore to avoid the noisy A82 on the opposite side. With the second biggest stretch of water in the Great Glen, the loch can be hard work for canoeists if the headwind is strong. Wild camping along the western shore is also popular during the summer while the Forestry Commission car park at Clunes is a good base for the day. For more information visit www.canoescotland.com

ANGLING

Forming part of the Caledonian Canal, Loch Lochy is managed by British Waterways and as such no permission to fish is required. Sunday fishing is also permitted. There is ample parking for fishermen along the busy A82 on the eastern shore while a more peaceful location can be reached via a forestry track at the northwestern corner of the loch near Kilfinnan. For more information contact Rod & Gun Shop, Fort William. Tel: 01397 702656 or visit the British Waterways website: www.britishwaterways.co.uk

BOAT TRIPS

Between April and October a constant procession of hire boats – cabin cruisers and yachts – and larger, more luxurious vessels with 5 Star on-board cabin accommodation and catering pass through Loch Lochy on their journey along the Caledonian Canal. Numerous companies offer boat hire or canal holidays along the canal, including the following:
www.calcycruisers.com
www.westhighlandsailing.com
www.fingal-cruising.co.uk
www.jacobite.co.uk

TOURIST INFORMATION AND ACCOMMODATION

Fort William Tourist Information Centre, 15 High Street, Fort William, Lochaber PH33 6DH Tel: +44 (845) 2255121
Website: www.visithighlands.com

Below *Overlooked by the peaks of Meall nan Dearcag and Sean Mheall a yacht slowly approaches Laggan Locks at the northeastern end of Loch Lochy. The Great Glen Way follows the shoreline in the distance.*

LOCH QUOICH

LOCH QUOICH VITAL STATISTICS

Max. length: 9.3mi
Surface area: 6.5mi²
Average depth: variable
Max. depth: c.45m
Water volume: variable

ORDNANCE SURVEY 1: 50,000 LANDRANGER MAP NO. 33

One of the most remote lochs in Scotland, Loch Quoich is set amidst a rugged, virtually uninhabited mountainous region between the Knoydart Peninsula and the Great Glen, a region renowned for its high rainfall. Now a giant reservoir for the Moriston-Garry hydro-electric scheme, the loch's water levels were raised by over 100ft during the building of a dam at its eastern end during the 1950s.

HISTORY
Traditionally the area around Loch Quoich and Loch Garry (see pages 106–109) to the east was the land ruled over by the powerful MacDonells of Glengarry. Prior to rising water levels, the shores around Loch Quoich also supported a few crofts and, later, the 19th century Glenquoich Lodge and its sporting estate. These buildings, along with the old road, the lodge and its rhododendron gardens and several islands all disappeared beneath the rising water levels in the 1950s. Their remains can still be seen on the rare occasions of long periods of drought and low water levels.

In the early 19th century one of these now submerged islands was the hideaway of one of Scotland's most notorious outlaws, Ewan MacPhee. A large man,

MacPhee never left his island hideaway unarmed, often sallying forth to do a bit of sheep stealing, poaching and illicit whisky distilling, safe in the knowledge that the local authorities lived in fear of him. The local population also lived in awe of this man who could apparently cast spells, tell fortunes and cure sick animals. In 1830 the Loch Quoich Estate was bought from the bankrupt MacDonells by the English millionaire politician, Edward Ellice. Ellice had made his money working for the Hudson's Bay Company in Canada and after his retirement from Parliament in 1834 entertained thousands of guests at his newly built Glenquoich Lodge and sporting estate. The painter Landseer was among his guests and he is reputed to have painted his famous *The Monarch of*

Above *Surrounded by a remote mountain wilderness, the western half of Loch Quoich is inaccessible by road. A track leads from the loch's western extremity through the Knoydart mountains to beautiful Barrisdale Bay. For more information about the Barrisdale Estate visit: www.barisdale.com*

Top *Built as part of the Moriston-Garry hydro-electric scheme in the 1950s, the dam across the eastern end of Loch Quoich is the largest rockfill dam in Scotland. When completed in 1957 it allowed water levels to rise by 100ft, submerging crofts, Glenquoich Lodge and much of the Loch Quoich Estate.*

Below *Built in the late 1950s to replace an older road flooded by rising water levels, this graceful steel bridge spans a northern arm of Loch Quoich and carries the single track road to Kinloch Hourn.*

the Glen a few miles to the northwest of Loch Quoich.

McPhee's sheep stealing (a capital offence at that time) continued unabated until the local authorities were forced to arrest him, but he died in prison in Fort William while awaiting trial. Ellice died in 1863 and was buried at Tor-na-Cairidh, a mound at the end of neighbouring Loch Garry. Strangely, although at opposite ends of the social spectrum, the outlaw MacPhee and the millionaire Ellice had coexisted peacefully around Loch Quoich for many years. Built in 1957 as part of the Moriston-Garry hydro-electric scheme, the dam at

the eastern end of Loch Quoich is the largest rockfill dam in Scotland – 1,050ft long and 125ft high. From here water flows down a tunnel to a power station on River Garry before outflowing to Loch Garry and finally to Loch Oich.

NATURAL HISTORY

Set in breathtaking scenery, the remote mountainsides around Loch Quoich are home to red deer and golden eagle. Sea eagle and osprey have also been seen around the loch in recent years. Four miles to the northwest of the loch lies the coastline of the rugged Knoydart Peninsula. The narrow, winding road from Loch Quoich ends at Kinloch Hourn where, out in Loch Beag, porpoise, seal and otter are regular sights.

Wild West Safaris operate wildlife trips to Loch Quoich and Kinloch Hourn. For more details Tel. +44 (0) 1809 501355 or visit: www.wildwestsafari.co.uk

WALKING, CLIMBING AND CYCLING

The minor road from the dam, along part of the north shore of the loch, to Kinloch Hourn in the Knoydart Peninsula sees little traffic so it is ideal for walkers or cyclists wishing to explore this remote and mountainous region. Away from this road stretch miles and miles of rugged mountain wilderness that should only be tackled by experienced and suitably equipped walkers and climbers. For Munro lovers Gleouraich (3,394ft) and Sgurr Mhaoraich (3,368ft) lie to the north while Sgurr Mor (3,289ft) and Sgurr nan Coireachan (3,125ft) lie to the south.

CANOEING AND KAYAKING

Much of the loch is inaccessible by road, so canoeing, kayaking and wild camping are the best way to experience this remote spot. Access can only be made from the minor road that follows part of the northern shoreline from the dam.

ANGLING AND BOAT HIRE

Excellent brown trout, ferox and Arctic char fishing. For permits and boat hire contact Tomdoun Lodge Hotel (see TOURIST INFORMATION AND ACCOMMODATION).

TOURIST INFORMATION AND ACCOMMODATION

Fort William Tourist Information Centre, 15 High Street, Fort Willam PH33 6DH
Tel. +44 (0) 845 2255121
Website: www.visithighlands.com

Tomdoun Lodge Hotel, Invergarry, Invernessshire, PH35 4HS
Tel. +44 (0)1809 511218
Website: www.tomdoun.com

Below *To the west of Loch Quoich the remote Knoydart Peninsula is famed for its mountain scenery, rugged coastline and wildlife. Reached along a footpath from Kinloch Hourn, this traditional cottage on the south shore of Loch Beag offers refreshments and accommodation for walkers en route to beautiful Barrisdale Bay.*

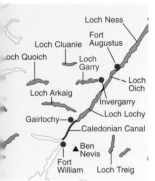

**LOCH GARRY
VITAL STATISTICS**
Max. length: 6.8mi
Surface area: 2.12mi²
Average depth: 49ft
Max. depth: 173ft
Water volume: 18
billion gallons

ORDNANCE
SURVEY 1: 50,000
LANDRANGER MAP
NO. 34

Above *Remnants of the ancient Caledonian Forest lie close to the southern shores of Loch Garry. Glen Garry Native Pine Wood is managed by the Forestry Commission and is home to many rare breeding bird species.*

Above *The bridge towards the western end of the loch is the starting point for forest trails through Glengarry Forest to Clunes, Laggan and Invergarry. Canoe, kayak and bike hire is available at Torr na Carraidh across the bridge.*

LOCH GARRY

Formed by glacial erosion during the last Ice Age and fed by the waters from Loch Quoich (see pages 102-105) via the River Garry, Loch Garry is surrounded by large areas of managed forest. Both lochs have been dammed at their eastern ends and form part of the Moriston-Garry hydro-electric scheme. Water is carried through a tunnel from Loch Garry to a power station on the banks of Loch Oich.

HISTORY

Located on an old drovers' road from Kinloch Hourn, Glen Garry was once the home of Clan MacDonnell of Glengarry with its ancestral seat at Invergarry Castle on the shores of nearby Loch Oich. Following years of bloody clan feuding the Battle of Morar was fought between Clan MacDonnell of Glengarry and Clan Mackenzie in 1602 (see pages 90-91). The chiefs of Glengarry were constantly in trouble - in 1649, Donald, the elderly 8th Chief of Glengarry, was denounced as a rebel for hiding fugitives from the Western Isles.

The MacDonnells of Glengarry were also a force to be reckoned with, raising 600 men to fight alongside Bonnie Prince Charlie during the Jacobite Rising of 1745-46. Battle honours included their victories at the Battle of Prestonpans in 1745 and the Battle of Falkirk in 1746.

The land around Loch Garry once supported a much bigger population than it does now. By 1815 the unpopular chief of the MacDonnells of Glengarry, Alaisdair Ranaldson MacDonell, had evicted many of the crofters from their land to make way for sheep farming. Repeated all over the Highlands and Islands, the Highland Clearances, as they became known, were a dark time for poverty stricken crofters and their familes, many of whom were forced to sail to North America to start a new life.

Today, while there is little tourism, trout farms and forestry management rub shoulders with sporting estates around the loch.

MYTHS AND LEGENDS

According to local legend a water spirit, or kelpie, inhabits the waters of Loch Garry. The story goes that seven children were playing on the banks of the River Garry when the kelpie came out of the water beside them. One of the children touched the creature and became stuck to it, followed by all of the other children until they were all stuck together. The kelpie then disappeared and all that was left of the children were their hearts floating on the loch. You have been warned!

Right *Set on the former drovers' road to Kinloch Hourn the Tomdoun Lodge Hotel lies midway between Loch Garry and Loch Quoich. Famous for its fishing, this hotel is an excellent base from which to explore the area.*

NATURAL HISTORY

To the south of the loch lies Glengarry Forest, its native pinewoods designated as part of the Caledonian Forest Reserve. Formed after the end of the last Ice Age the Caledonian Forest once covered a large part of northern Scotland and was home to brown bear, lynx, grey wolf and elk. Now only 1% of the forest remains and this is found at 35 isolated locations, including Glengarry Forest.

What remains of the forest supports a wide range of bird species not found anywhere else in Britain - these include the capercaillie, goldeneye, redwing, crested tit and golden eagle. Mammal species include mountain hare, pine marten, red deer, red squirrel and wildcat.

Glen Garry Native Pine Wood is managed by the Forestry Commission and is surrounded by other tree species including broadleaves and conifers.

WALKING AND CYCLING

The area around Loch Garry is ideal walking and mountain biking country - the chances of bumping into anyone else are pretty remote. The many trails in Glengarry Forest can be accessed either from several Forestry Commission car parks alongside the A87 west of Invergarry or from the minor road about three-quarters of the way down the north shore of the loch and then by foot

across a bridge to Torr na Carraidh. The Daingean Trail, reached from the Trail car park on the A87 five miles west of Invergarry, is an easy walk that explores the original settlement of Daingean. The Gleann Laogh Trail to the native pinewoods of Glengarry Forest is a Forestry Commission waymarked walk that starts at the White Bridge car park two miles west of Invergarry. For more serious walkers the footpath to Ben Tee (2,955ft) can be reached from Alt na Cailliche car park in the Glen Garry Native Pine Wood.

Many of the forest trails around Glen Garry make ideal mountain bike rides while the minor road along the north shore of the loch, reached off the A87 five miles west of Invergarry, is an ideal start for a day's cycling to Loch Quoich and the sea at remote Kinloch Hourn. Refreshments are available at tea rooms here while a stop can be made on the return journey at the Tomdoun Hotel.

CANOEING AND KAYAKING
Access is from the minor road along the north shore. Just over a mile from the A87 there is a small slipway which is also used by local fish farms. Canoe, kayak and bike hire are available at Torr na Carraidh, reached across a bridge towards the western end of the loch.

ANGLING AND BOAT HIRE

Loch Garry is populated by pike, brown trout, salmon and ferox trout. Fishing is by way of bank or boat and the season is from 15 March to 6 October. For permits, boat and tackle hire Tel. +44 (0)1809 511232. Permits can also be obtained from the Tomdoun Hotel. Tel. +44 (0)1809 511218. This hostelry is renowned for its fishing and also offers stalking, shooting and mountain biking.

TOURIST INFORMATION AND ACCOMMODATION

Fort William Tourist Information Centre, 15 High Street, Fort Willam PH33 6DH Tel. +44 (0) 845 2255121 Website: www.visithighlands.com

Fort Augustus Tourist Information Centre, The Car Park, Fort Augustus, PH32 4DD. Tel. +44 (0) 1320 36636 or visit: www.fortaugustus.org

Tomdoun Hotel, Invergarry, Invernessshire, PH35 4HS Tel. +44 (0)1809 511218 Website: www.tomdoun.com

Below *From the viewpoint on the A87 high above Loch Garry, the loch's outline has an appearance similar to a map of Scotland. The bridge across the loch allows foot and mountain bike access from the north shore road to Glengarry Forest trails.*

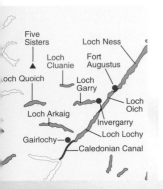

LOCH CLUANIE
VITAL STATISTICS
Max. length: 7mi
Surface area: 4mi²
Average depth:
variable
Max. depth: 45m
Water volume: variable

ORDNANCE
SURVEY 1: 50,000
LANDRANGER
MAPS NOS. 33/34

LOCH CLUANIE

Dammed at its eastern end, bleak and treeless Loch Cluanie was formed as a reservoir for the North of Scotland Hydro-Electric Board's Glenmoriston project after World War II. Loch Loyne, to the south of Loch Cluanie, was also formed in this way. Following completion of the dam, the rising waters of Loch Cluanie swallowed up two smaller natural lochs - Loch Lundie and Loch Beagh. Water outflow from the loch is controlled via a three-mile tunnel to an underground power station at Ceannacroc. From here the water discharges into the River Moriston before flowing into Loch Ness.

Loch Cluanie also features a natural phenomenon known as the Cluanie Curtain. Regularly seen by motorists driving along the lochside A87, this raincloud is swept up the loch by the prevailing westerly wind.

HISTORY

For hundreds of years a cattle drovers' road, the famous 'Road to the Isles', passed through the area on its long and tortuous route from the Isle of Skye to the lowlands of Scotland. Now marked as a track on modern maps, a section of this once-important road can be traced northwards from Tomdoun Lodge (to the west of Loch Garry; see pages 106-109) to the western end of Loch Cluanie at the Cluanie Inn, en route disappearing

Above and below *Built as part of the Glenmoriston hydro-electric scheme the dam at the eastern end of Loch Cluanie is 2,214ft long and 131ft high. At times of prolonged rainfall the waters of the loch will nearly lap the top of the dam but during dry periods (below) the original physical features of the glen become exposed.*

beneath the waters of Loch Loyne. The current A87 along the north shore of Loch Cluanie, in parts following the course of an old military road from Fort Augustus, replaced this ancient road during the construction of the two reservoirs after World War II.

Five miles to the west of Loch Cluanie, Glen Shiel was the scene of a bloody battle in 1719 between 850 British government troops and a 1,000-strong army of Jacobites and Spaniards – the latter having landed at Eilean Donan Castle at the entrance to Loch Duich. The result was a victory for the goverment forces and ended yet another Jacobite rebellion. A mountain close to the site of the battle was later named Sgurr nan Spainteach (The Peak of the Spaniards).

Following the defeat of the Jacobites at the Battle of Culloden in 1746, Bonnie Prince Charlie hid in a cave above Cluanie after escaping from Skye. Despite a reward of £30,000 for his capture (an enormous amount at that time) he was protected by the 'seven men of Glenmoriston' before making his way back to France via the Outer Hebrides.

The present-day Cluanie Inn at the western end of the loch has been providing sustenance and beds for weary travellers along the 'Road to Skye' since the 19th century. For more details contact the Cluanie Inn, Glenmoriston, Inverness IV63 7YW. Tel. +44 (0) 1320 340238 or visit: www.cluanieinn.com)

NATURAL HISTORY

Surrounded by mountains, including a group of three Munros to the north, the treeless shores around Loch Cluanie can be a bleak place. This is red deer and golden eagle country although sea eagles are occasionally seen over the loch.

WALKING, CYCLING AND CLIMBING

Too numerous to mention, there are 21 Munros to be found a short distance to the north and west of the loch. These include such classics as the Glen Shiel Ridge, Five Sisters of Kintail, Aonach air Chrith and A'Chrolaig.

For walkers and mountain bikers the old 'Road to the Isles' drovers' road can be followed for seven miles from the west end of the loch near the Cluanie Inn, from where it strikes off in a

southeasterly direction towards Loch Loyne. Here it disappears beneath the waters of this reservoir before reappearing on the south shore.

CANOEING AND KAYAKING

Difficult to access due to the dam at eastern end and the busy A87 on the northern shore. Launching may be possible at the western end.

ANGLING

Fishing is by way of bank or boat for brown trout. The season is from 15 March to 6 October. For more information and permits contact Cluanie Lodge, Glenmoriston (Tel. +44 (0) 340262) or Cluanie Inn (Tel. +44 (0) 1320 340238). Boat hire is not available. The loch is also well known for pike fishing for which no permit is required.

TOURIST INFORMATION AND ACCOMMODATION

Fort Augustus Tourist Information Centre, The Car Park, Fort Augustus, Highland PH32 4DD
Tel +44 (0) 1320 36636
or visit: www.fortaugustus.org

LOCH OICH
VITAL STATISTICS
Max. length: 4mi
Surface area: 1mi²
Average depth: 72ft
Max. depth: 154ft
Water volume: 12
billion gallons

ORDNANCE
SURVEY 1: 50,000
LANDRANGER MAP
NO. 34

Below *Waters at the northern end of Loch Oich flow into the River Oich over a weir before outflowing into Loch Ness. Opened in 1822, the Caledonian Canal links the two lochs by way of a series of man-made cuts and seven locks. The 62-mile Great Glen Way long distance path follows the western side of the canal to Fort Augustus.*

LOCH OICH

Loch Oich lies along the Great Glen Fault which runs diagonally through Scotland from Inverness down to Loch Linnhe and continues on into northwest Ireland through Donegal Bay. In geological terms it is called a strike-slip fault, formed around 400 million years ago during a period of intense volcanic activity when the Baltic and Laurentia tectonic plates collided.

As with other Scottish lochs, Loch Oich was scoured and shaped by the movement of glaciers during the last major Ice Age to cover Europe which began around two million years ago and ended around 11,500 years ago.

Much smaller than its neighbours, Loch Oich is connected to Loch Lochy in the south by a man-made cut of the Caledonian Canal. To the north its outflow to Loch Ness is via the River Oich. The waters of Loch Quoich and Loch Garry to the west have been harnessed for hydro-electric generation while their outflow, the River Garry, enters Loch Oich on its western shore near Invergarry.

HISTORY

Located on a strategic knoll known as Raven's Rock on the west bank of Loch Oich, Invergarry Castle was once the seat of the powerful Chiefs of the MacDonnells of Glengarry, a branch of Clan Donald. For years the castle was the scene of violent clan feuding which

culminated in raids by the Clan Mackenzie in 1602. In 1654, during the Civil War, it was again attacked – this time by Cromwellian forces led by General Monck who burned the castle to the ground.

Rebuilt to its present design around 1660 the unfortunate castle was then subjected to further attacks and changes of ownership over the next century. Occupied by Jacobites from 1688, the building was seized by Government forces in 1692 until it was retaken during the First Rebellion of 1715. A year later it was reoccupied by English troops and burned down again. Subsequently repaired, the castle finally reverted to its rightful owner, the Chief of the MacDonells of Glengarry, in 1731. Held by Jacobite forces during the Second Rebellion of 1745 it was also visited by Bonnie Prince Charlie before and after

the Battle of Culloden. Following the battle the castle was finally reduced to its present ruinous state by the Duke of Cumberland's troops.

Set in the grounds of Glengarry Castle Hotel, Invergarry Castle is now the subject of a fund raising appeal to make its structure safe.

Erected in 1812, the Well of Heads monument alongside the A82 south of Invergarry commemorates a grueseome episode in local history. In 1663, during a quarrel, two sons of the Chief of MacDonnell were murdered by an uncle and his six sons. In retaliation they were all beheaded and their heads presented to the Chief in Invergarry Castle.

The only railway built into the Great Glen was opened from Spean Bridge to Fort Augustus in 1903. Never a financial success, the line closed to passengers in 1933 and completely in 1946. Its

trackbed, now part of the Great Glen Way long distance path, can be traced along the east shore of the loch.

MYTHS AND LEGENDS
Along with its two neighbours, it is only fitting that Loch Oich is apparently inhabited by a monster. Sightings of a dog-headed serpent, known as Dobhar-chu, date back to the 19th century and, although it is supposed to have drowned a boy who hitched a ride on its back, there has never been any firm evidence of its existence.

Below inset *Now closed to road traffic the Bridge of Oich over the River Oich near Aberchalder was built as a suspension bridge in 1854. It was replaced by a modern concrete bridge further upstream in 1932.*

Left *Set in the grounds of Glengarry Castle Hotel, Invergarry Castle was once the seat of the Chiefs of the MacDonells of Glengarry, a branch of Clan Donald. Today, its ruins are considered unsafe for exploration.*

NATURAL HISTORY

The area around the loch is particularly rich in wildlife - the red squirrel and the pine marten, the latter best seen at dusk when looking for food, are both popular with visitors. In spring the woodland around Leitirfearn, half way down the east shore of the loch, has a colourful carpet of primrose and dog violet. Loch Oich, along with the other lochs in the Great Glen, becomes the spawning grounds for migrating salmon each autumn. The baby salmon, known as fingerlings, stay in the loch for two years before migrating out to sea.

WALKING AND CYCLING

The Great Glen Way long distance path runs along an old railway trackbed on the east bank of Loch Oich. Ideal for both walkers and cyclists this section of the path between the Activity Centre near Laggan and Aberchalder is traffic-free and level. Suitable for mountain bikes, National Cycle Network Route 78 runs parallel to the A82 through woodland between South Laggan and Aberchalder on the west side of the loch.

CANOEING AND KAYAKING

Monster Activities (see below) provide instruction, courses and hire facilities for kayaks and Canadian canoes from their Activity Centre near the Laggan swing bridge. A popular wild camping site is at Leitirfearn on the east shore of the loch.

ANGLING AND BOAT HIRE

Loch Oich is populated by pike, brown trout, ferox trout, sea trout, salmon, eels and roach. Permits are available from local hotels and boat hire can be obtained from Monster Activities, Great Glen Water Park, South Laggan. Tel. 07710 540398 or visit: www.monsteractivities.com

TOURIST INFORMATION AND ACCOMMODATION

Fort William Tourist Information Centre, 15 High Street, Fort Willam PH33 6DH
Tel. +44 (0) 845 2255121
Website: www.visithighlands.com

Fort Augustus Tourist Information Centre, The Car Park, Fort Augustus, Highland PH32 4DD
Tel +44 (0) 1320 36636
or visit: www.fortaugustus.org

Below *Walkers and cyclists travelling along the Great Glen Way pass the site of Invergarry railway station which had a short working life on the Spean Bridge to Fort Augustus railway. Opened in 1903 the line never fulfilled its promotors' wild dreams and was closed to passengers in 1933. Goods traffic continued until 1946 when the line was closed. Its trackbed along the east shore of Loch Oich now forms part of the Great Glen Way.*

CALEDONIAN CANAL

Prior to the building of the Caledonian Canal along the Great Glen - a geological fault in the Earth's crust - in the 19th century, sailing ships had to make the long and dangerous journey from the northeast of Scotland to the southwest via Pentland Firth, Cape Wrath and The Minch. By the time of the first survey for the canal by James Watt in 1773, the Highland region of Scotland was already suffering from the effects of the notorious 'Clearances' - the result for many people was unemployment or an unknown future in North America. The building of the canal therefore had two major benefits for the region: a safer and shorter passage for ships and much-needed employment for the local population.

The canal was authorised by an Act of Parliament in 1803. The famous canal engineer Thomas Telford, aided by William Jessop, was appointed to oversee the project. Funded by the Government, costs were reckoned to be just under £500,000 and the schedule for completion was seven years - in the end both of these were wildly underestimated.

Unlike other canals in the UK, the 62-mile Caledonian Canal from Inverness to Corpach, near Fort William, was made up of short man-made cuts linking the three freshwater lochs down the Great Glen - lochs Ness, Oich and Lochy. The man-made cuts included 29 locks, four aqueducts and 10 bridges. William Jessop died in 1814, difficulties were experienced with both the construction and the work force and the canal finally opened in 1822 - 12 years late and £436,000 over budget. By then steam ships were being introduced which were too large to travel along the canal and the project was looking like a white elephant. Fortunately, the coming of the railways to the Highlands, royal patronage and the subsequent increase in visitors to the region saved the canal. Steamboat services became a regular feature and east coast fishing boats were using it as a short

Below *Carrying the A82 across the Caledonian Canal, the swing bridge at Aberchalder slowly opens to allow passage of a ship travelling from Loch Oich. The canal became part of British Waterways in 1962 following which locks and swing bridges were mechanised.*

Below *The* Lord of the Glens *slowly emerges from Gairlochy Top Lock on its leisurely journey from Inverness to Corpach. Designed to squeeze into the canal's locks, this cruise ship can carry up to 54 passengers in total luxury.*

cut to their fishing grounds off the west coast. Heavily used during World War I, the canal is now a Scheduled Ancient Monument and, following recent major restoration of its locks by British Waterways, its future seems assured.

Today, over half a million visitors are attracted to the canal each year. Apart from its continuing all-year-round use by fishing boats it is also used by a steady procession of yachts, motor boats and small luxury cruise ships during the summer.

Below *The path alongside the five-mile man-made cut between Loch Oich at Aberchalder and Loch Ness at Fort Augustus now forms part of the Great Glen Way long distance path and Route 78 of the National Cycle Network.*

Below *Fishing boats heading for Loch Ness and the North Sea make their leisurely progress through the five staircase locks at Fort Augustus.*

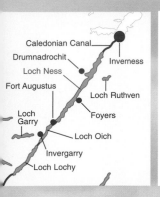

LOCH NESS VITAL STATISTICS
Max. length: 24mi
Surface area: 21.8mi²
Average depth: 433ft
Max. depth:754ft
Water volume: 1.64 trillion gallons

ORDNANCE SURVEY 1: 50,000 LANDRANGER MAPS NOS. 26/34

Below *The ruins of 13th century Urquhart Castle near Drumnadrochit stand guard over the still waters of Loch Ness. In 1940, an RAF Wellington bomber ditched in the loch after engine failure, all but one of the crew survived - 45 years later the plane was raised from the water and restored. Sadly, while breaking the world water speed record in 1952, John Cobb was killed on the loch while travelling at over 200mph in his speedboat 'Crusader'.*

LOCH NESS

Loch Ness lies along the Great Glen Fault which runs diagonally through Scotland from Inverness down to Loch Linnhe and continues on into northwest Ireland through Donegal Bay. In geological terms it is called a strike-slip fault, formed around 400 million years ago during a period of intense volcanic activity when the Baltic and Laurentia tectonic plates collided.

As with other Scottish lochs, Loch Ness was scoured and shaped by the movement of glaciers during the last major Ice Age to cover Europe which began around two million years ago and ended around 11,500 years ago.

Although Loch Ness is the second largest loch in Scotland by surface area its depth makes it the largest by volume of water - only Loch Morar is deeper. At its northern end the loch outflows via the River Ness into the Beauly Firth at Inverness. At its southern end it is linked to Loch Oich via the River Oich at Fort Augustus. The waters of Loch Ness are particularly murky due their high peat content brought down from the hillsides.

HISTORY

Cutting diagonally through the Scottish Highlands the Great Glen has been an important strategic route since the early years of human activity in the region around 4,000 years ago. By the first millennium, northern Pictish tribes had settled in the Glen and a crannog – an artificial island known as Cherry Island– dating from this period can be seen in the loch near Fort Augustus.

By the latter half of the 6th century the northern Picts were being visited by St Columba and his followers from Iona. Conversion to Christianity soon followed but by the early 13th century the Great Glen was in great turmoil following revolts against the English crown.

Dating from this period, the ruins of Urquhart Castle on Strone Point half way up the western shore of the loch near Drumnadrochit stand testimony to this turbulent time. Over the following three centuries the castle changed hands several times, firstly in 1296 when it was seized by Edward I of England. In 1545, while under the ownership of the Grants, it was captured by the MacDonalds, then, in 1644, it was recaptured by a Covenanter army allied to English Parliamentary forces during the English Civil War. The final chapter in the castle's turbulent history came in 1692 when it was reduced to rubble by English troops to stop it falling into Jacobite hands. The castle has remained ruined since then and is now owned by the National Trust of Scotland. For more information visit: www.nts.org.uk

For centuries before the advent of the modern roads we know today, the communities along the shores of Loch Ness depended on boat transport to maintain contact with the outside world.

The first road to be built along the Great Glen actually preceded the building of the Caledonian Canal. Following the Jacobite Rebellion in 1715 the British government sent Major General Wade to Scotland where he recommended the building of barracks, bridges and roads to help bring stability to the region. Between 1725 and 1737 Wade directed the building of 250 miles of road, 40 bridges and garrisons at Ruthven, Fort George, Fort Augustus and Fort William. The road linking these garrisons was built along the eastern side of the Great Glen and its route is clearly marked on modern maps.

The Great Glen was transformed into a 'super highway' in the early 19th century by the building of the Caledonian Canal (see pages 116–117). Providing much-needed employment in this depressed area and engineered by Thomas Telford, the 62-mile canal linked Inverness with Corpach near Fort William via Lochs Dochfour, Ness, Oich

Below *Owned by the National Trust for Scotland, Urquhart Castle has lain in ruins since it was destroyed by English forces in 1692 to stop it falling into the hands of the Jacobites. It is now one of the most popular tourist attractions in Scotland.*

and Lochy. Opened throughout in 1822, the man-made cuts between the lochs included the building of 29 locks of which the most dramatic are the five at Fort Augustus. Sadly the canal never lived up to expectations because by the time it was completed modern sea-going ships were too large to use it. The canal's steamboat services, however, were a vital link along the Great Glen until the advent of modern roads and certainly assisted in the growth of tourism.

Despite several ill-conceived proposals that never got off the drawing board railways had a minimal impact on the communities along Loch Ness. The intense rivalry between the Highland Railway at Inverness and the North British Railway at Fort William

meant that railway development along the Great Glen into each other's territory never saw the light of day. The only railway actually built, from Spean Bridge to Fort Augustus, was a white elephant from its opening in 1903, costing its promotors vast amounts of money with no chance of a return on their investment. The line closed to passengers in 1933 and completely in 1946.

Industry came to the eastern shore of Loch Ness in 1895 when the North British Aluminium Company opened an aluminium processor at Foyers. The large amount of electricity required for aluminium production was generated by

hydro-electricity using the fast-flowing waters of the River Foyers. Although aluminium production ceased in 1967 hydro-electric power is still generated here and fed into the National Grid.

MYTHS AND LEGENDS

Along with the Himalayan Yeti and the North American Big Foot, the Loch Ness Monster must rate as one of the most famous creatures in the world which many people claim to have seen but which may not exist.

Various unidentified creatures have apparently been seen in and around Loch Ness since the time of St Columba in the 6th century AD but to this day one has never been reliably photographed or caught - live or dead. Many claims and photographs have eventually turned out to be hoaxes at the worst or unreliable at the best but this still doesn't stop thousands of tourists descending on Loch Ness each year in the hope of seeing the fabled monster. For sceptics or believers a visit to the Loch Ness Exhibition Centre at Drumnadrochit is a must. For more details visit: www.lochness.com

The Official Loch Ness Monster website (www.nessie.co.uk) also features many fascinating stories of sightings.

NATURAL HISTORY

Away from the busy A82 and the tourist hordes waiting for a glimpse of the 'monster', the Great Glen with its varied habitats ranging from woodland, moorland and shoreline is home to a rich variety of wildlife. While sika, fallow and roe deer, badger, feral goat, fox, brown hare and weasel are fairly common sights the red squirrel and the elusive pine

Above *Completed in 1822, the 62-mile Caledonian Canal links the three major lochs in the Great Glen via man-made cuts and 29 locks. The five locks at Fort Augustus, a major tourist attraction, are busy with the comings and goings of cruisers, yachts and fishing boats during the summer months.*

Below *Apart from Loch Morar, Loch Ness is the deepest loch in Scotland. It is also the largest by volume of water and contains more fresh water than all of the lakes in England and Wales combined. Some say that the entire population of the world could fit into it while others are just happy to enjoy its breathtaking natural beauty.*

marten can also be spotted with patience.

Birdlife around the loch is prolific - in woodlands and gardens the great spotted woodpecker, siskin finch, and treecreeper are common visitors while raptors such as buzzard, red kite, merlin, peregrine falcon, kestrel, sparrow hawk and even the rare osprey can be seen in the skies above. Red legged partridge, pheasant and red grouse are also a common sight in the surrounding woods and moorland.

In the winter the waters of Loch Ness are home to goldeneye, cormorant and goosander while grey herons and mute swans are regular visitors.

The deep and murky waters of Loch Ness are also home to a wide variety of fish including European eel, pike, stickleback, lamphrey, minnow, native brown trout, Arctic char, sea trout and Atlantic salmon.

WALKING AND CYCLING

There are many waymarked walks and cycle trails in the Loch Ness area, ranging from gentle strolls to demanding hikes and hill walks. Information on these walks and trails can be obtained from local tourist information centres. Dynamic maps showing walks around Loch Ness can be found at: www.visitlochness.com

The Balnain Bike Park, five miles west of Drumnadrochit is managed by the Forestry Commission. For mountain biking and information on the world famous Great Glen Mountain Bike Trails visit: www.greatglentrails.com

Both walkers and cyclists are also well catered for by the 73-mile Great Glen Way Long Distance Path

which runs from Inverness to Fort William alongside Loch Ness. For more information visit: www.greatglenway.com

CANOEING, KAYAKING AND SAILING

With its extreme depth, prevailing southwesterly winds and waves up to a three feet in height, Loch Ness can be a dangerous place in an open canoe. The sensible advice is to keep close to one of the shores and avoid crossing over the middle of the loch. For more information on canoeing visit: www.canoescotland.com

Sailing is also popular on the loch and yachts, along with luxury motor cruisers, can be hired from West Highland Sailing & Cruises: www.westhighlandsailing.com

BOAT TRIPS

Between April and October a constant procession of hire boats - cabin cruisers and yachts - and larger, more luxurious vessels with 5 Star on-board cabin accommodation and catering pass through Loch Ness on their journey along the Caledonian Canal. Numerous companies offer boat hire or canal holidays along the canal, including the following:
www.caleycruisers.com
www.westhighlandsailing.com
www.fingal-cruising.co.uk
www.jacobite.co.uk

Several companies offer sightseeing trips around Loch Ness. For more information contact local tourist information centres.

ANGLING AND BOAT HIRE

The Great Glen is laced with rivers and lochs where you can fly-fish for salmon and trout. Fishing for brown trout or salmon on Loch Ness is by way of bank or boat. The season is from 15 March to 6 October for brown trout and from January 15 to October for salmon. Tourist information centres and hotels can provide information on locations, permits, fishing rights and boat hire. For information visit: www.fortaugustus.org

TOURIST INFORMATION AND ACCOMMODATION

Fort Augustus Tourist Information Centre, The Car Park, Fort Augustus, Highland PH32 4DD
Tel. +44 (0) 1320 36636
Website: www.fortaugustus.org
Inverness Tourist Information Centre, Castle Wynd, Inverness IV2 3BJ
Tel. + 44 (0) 1463 234353
Website: www.visitscotland.com

LOCH RUTHVEN

Despite being only 12 miles south of Inverness, Loch Ruthven is set in a fairly remote location reached along winding minor roads from the B851 or the B862. Famous as the site of an important RSPB reserve visited by the rare Slavonian grebe, the loch has rocky margins apart from an area of marshland at its western end and is surrounded by considerable stands of bottle sedge and birch woods around its shoreline.

HISTORY

A crannog, or small man-made island, at the western end of Loch Ruthven is evidence of human activity around the loch over 1,000 years ago. It was probably linked to the shore by a causeway. Not much is left now apart from a low mound which is inhabited by a colony of common gulls. A low knoll named Tom Buidhe, nearby on the south shore may also be the site of an early dwelling or cultivation plot.

Loch Ruthven was the scene of a murder in the late 15th century when Hugh Fraser, the 1st Fraser of Foyers, killed his half-brother, John Fraser of Lovat, in a duel. Hugh then fled to France where he had close connections.

During the 20th century Loch Ruthven was recognised as an important ecological site and received special protection when it was classified as a Site of Special Scientific Interest, Special Area of Conservation, Special Protection Area, Ramsar site and partly as an RSPB nature reserve. A hide was opened on the loch's side by the latter organisation in 1989.

NATURAL HISTORY

First and foremost Loch Ruthven is known as the site of an important RSPB nature reserve and is particularly famous for its breeding population of rare and colourful Slavonian grebe, accounting for 20% of the UK population, in early spring. Other birds that can be spotted from the lochside hide at various times of the year are osprey, black-throated and red-throated diver, goldeneye and red-breasted merganser. Birdlife around the loch includes peregrine falcon, woodcock, ring ouzel, short-eared owl, winchat, lesser redpoll, wheatear and cuckoo. Visitors can use a small car park at the site. For more details visit: www.rspb.org.uk

The loch's clear waters are also home to wild brown trout and stickleback and the dense birch woods that encircle the loch are home to several rare plants including the bog and coralroot orchids.

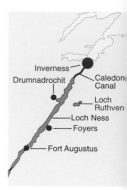

LOCH RUTHVEN
VITAL STATISTICS
Max. length: 2.5mi
Surface area: 0.77mi^2
Average depth: 23ft
Max. depth: 33ft
Water volume: 3 billion gallons

ORDNANCE SURVEY 1: 50,000 LANDRANGER MAP NO. 35

WALKING AND CLIMBING

A 500yd-long trail in the RSPB reserve at the eastern end of the loch leads from the small car park to a lochside hide. A longer 11-mile return walk from Loch Ruthven northwards to Loch Duntelchaig passes through forest and moorland offering good views across to Ben Wyvis and along Strathnairn. The rocky outcrops of Stac Gorm (1,410ft), immediately to the south of Loch Ruthven, beckon the more adventurous walker and climber.

ANGLING AND BOAT HIRE

Loch Ruthven is reckoned to be one of the best wild brown trout fishing lochs in Scotland. Fishing is by rowing boat only. The season for wild brown trout is 15 March to 6 October. For further information and permits contact J Graham & Co, 37-39 Castle Street, Inverness IV2 3DU.
Tel. +44 (0) 1463 222757
Website: www.grahamsonline.co.uk.

CANOEING AND KAYAKING

Paddling canoes or kayaks is a great way to see wildlife on Loch Ruthven but users should respect the breeding ground of the Slavonian grebe at the eastern end.

TOURIST INFORMATION AND ACCOMMODATION

Inverness Tourist Information Centre, Castle Wynd, Inverness IV2 3BJ
Tel. + 44 (0) 1463 234353
Website: www.visitscotland.com

Left and right *Remote Loch Ruthven is classified as a Site of Special Scientific Interest, Special Area of Conservation, Special Protection Area, Ramsar site and partly an RSPB nature reserve. Safe from natural predators, the rare Slavonian grebe breeds here during the spring and summer months.*

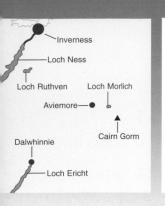

LOCH MORLICH
VITAL STATISTICS
Max. length: 1.2mi
Surface area: 0.77mi²
Average depth: 23ft
Max. depth: 39ft
Water volume: 3 billion
gallons

ORDNANCE
SURVEY 1: 50,000
LANDRANGER MAP
NO. 36

LOCH MORLICH

Below *Overlooked by the snowclad Cairngorm Mountains, the crystal clear waters of Loch Morlich are popular with watersports enthusiasts.*

Famous for its curving and pine-fringed sandy beach, Loch Morlich is located in the Glenmore Forest Park midway between the all-year-round resort village of Aviemore and the Cairn Gorm ski-slopes. It is fed by the waters of numerous tumbling burns that flow down into Glen More from the northern slopes of the Cairngorm Mountains, outflowing along the River Luineag to the River Spey at Aviemore. The loch and the surrounding area were used by the British Special Operations Executive for commando training during World War II and is probably the most popular outdoor activity location in Scotland.

HISTORY

By the 19th century much of the ancient Caledonian pinewoods that covered Glen More had been cut down and replaced by sheep and cattle grazing. Until the

opening of the Highland Railway's main line between Perth and Inverness in 1863, nearby Aviemore was just a small isolated village which had only existed since the 17th century. The coming of the railway transformed the area and its popularity as a holiday destination grew, no doubt helped by Queen Victoria who regularly visited the area. The nearby Cairngorm Mountains were also a magnet for explorers, climbers and geologists – the latter searching for a semi-precious gold-coloured stone that was once found here.

What was left of Glenmore Forest was purchased by the newly-formed Forestry Commission in 1923 and half of its 8,600 acres were replanted with foreign varieties of conifer for commercial use. In 1948, Glenmore Forest became the second forest park to be created by the Commission.

During World War II, Loch Morlich and the surrounding area was chosen as a site for a commando school by the Special Operations Executive. Among those who received training here were units of the Norwegian Independent Army (Kompani Linge) because the loch, suurounding mountains and deep snow in winter were considered to be similar to that found in Norway.

Special Training School 26, or STS26 for short, requisitioned three Victorian hunting lodges in the area and went on to train at least 400 Norwegian agents in the art of mountain warfare. The most famous were those trained to attack the heavy water facility at the Vermork Norsk Hydro plant in the town of Rjukan in Telemark, Norway. This event, known as Operation Grouse, was later immortalised, albeit with considerable

Below *Cradled by the Glenmore Forest Park and fringed by sandy beaches, Loch Morlich and the surrounding area are an all-year-round attraction for walkers, mountain bike riders, orienteers, watersports enthusiasts and anglers.*

factual licence, in the 1965 film *The Heroes of Telemark* featuring Kirk Douglas and Richard Harris.

After the war, one of the lodges used by STS26, Glenmore Lodge, became a hostel for the Central Council for Physical Education and later Scotland's National Outdoor Training Centre. With heavy snowfall in the winter, Coire Cas on the nearby northern slopes of Cairn Gorm, soon became a popular destination for skiers. An access road was built from Loch Morlich to the ski slopes, and the first chair lift, known as the White Lady, opened in 1961. To cope with ever increasing demand from skiers to reach the slopes, a funicular railway was opened to the Ptarmigan restaurant and viewpoint in 2001.

NATURAL HISTORY

Loch Morlich and the surrounding area is located in Glenmore Forest Park, part of the Cairngorms National Park. The forest holds one of the few remaining stands of ancient Caledonian pinewood in Scotland. Only about 197 acres of this pristine pine, juniper and birch woodland survive in Glenmore although work to restore another 2,500 acres is underway. Away from the busy northern shore of the loch (over a quarter of a million people visit the area each year), the surrounding forest is home to a wide range of animal and bird life, while a herd of reindeer roam freely in the grounds of Reindeer House to the east of the loch. Loch Morlich has been awarded a Rural Beach Award for its excellent water quality – the first and only freshwater inland loch to have gained this award in Scotland.

WALKING, CYCLING AND ORIENTEERING

With one of the finest setting in Scotland – surrounded by forests and fringed by beaches – the circuit of Loch Morlich is a very popular walk. Nature trails abound in the surrounding forest. For the more adventurous the Munros of the Cairngorm range beckon from the south. Cyclists are also well-catered for with a dedicated cycle track from Aviemore and various forest mountain bike trails. Loch Morlich Watersports (see WATERSPORTS) organise mountain bike tours around Glenmore Forest. The National Orienteering Centre is based at Glenmore Lodge - for more details visit: www.scottish-orienteering.org
Note: Forestry Commission car parks around the loch are pay-and-display.

WATERSPORTS

Approved by the Scottish Canoe Association and the Royal Yachting Association, Loch Morlich Watersports provides lessons and hire facilities for canoeing, kayaking, sailing and windsurfing. For more details of their comprehensive operation contact Loch Morlich Watersports:
Tel. +44 (0) 1479 861221
Website: www.lochmorlich.com

FISHING AND BOAT HIRE

Fishing is by way of bank or boat for brown trout and coarse species such as pike. The brown trout season is 15 March to 6 October. Fishing permits and boat hire available from Loch Morlich Watersports (see above).

TOURIST INFORMATION AND ACCOMMODATION

Aviemore Tourist Information Centre, Unit 7, Grampian Road, Aviemore, Highland PH22 1RH
Tel. +44 (0) 845 2255121
Website: www.visitscotland.com

NORTHWEST SCOTLAND

Loch Coruisk
Loch Maree
Loch Assynt
Loch Shin

LOCH CORUISK

**LOCH CORUISK
VITAL STATISTICS**
Max. length: 1.74mi
Surface area: 0.5mi^2
Average depth: 82ft
Max. depth: 115ft
Water volume: 7 billion
gallons

ORDNANCE
SURVEY 1: 50,000
LANDRANGER MAP
No. 32

Below *Loch Coruisk's remoteness and wild, natural beauty have attracted writers, poets and artists for several centuries. Following his visit in 1814 Sir Walter Scott described the loch in these lines from his poem* The Lord of the Isles:

> *'Rarely human eye has known
> A scene so stern as that dread lake,
> With its dark ledge of barren stone...'*

Lord Tennyson described it as the 'wildest scene in the Highlands'. Its Gaelic name of Coire Uisg means 'Cauldron of Waters'.

Loch Coruisk lies at the foot of the Black Cuillin mountains in the Isle of Skye. At its southern end the loch outflows through a short stream to the sea loch of Loch Scavaig. Probably the most dramatic mountain range in Britain, the Cuillin Hills are all that remains from a period of extreme volcanic activity that occurred during the Palaeogenic period, 65–1.6 million years ago. At this time tectonic plates were moving apart – America moving westwards and Europe moving eastwards. The growing split between them formed the Atlantic Ocean that we know today.

Attracting climbers and walkers from around the world, the tall, foreboding and jagged peaks of the Black Cuillins are mainly composed of gabbro, a dark coarse-grained rock formed when molten magma is trapped beneath the Earth's surface, crystallising during cooling.

Our understanding of Skye's igneous rocks was made possible by the work of 19th century geologists such as Archibald Geikie and John Judd. However, the most significant contribution was made by Dr Alfred Harker who conducted detailed surveying and geological studies of the west of Scotland and the Isle of Skye for the Geological Survey of Scotland in the early 20th century.

HISTORY AND CULTURE

Miles from civilisation, remote Loch Coruisk never witnessed the bloodshed and violence often witnessed in other parts of Scotland. The only event worthy of note was the Battle

of Coire na Creiche which was fought in 1601 on the northern slopes of Bruach na Frithe, two miles north of the loch, between the MacDonalds of Sleat and the MacLeods of Dunvegan. In this, the final clan battle on Skye, the winners were the MacDonalds.

Loch Coruisk's remoteness and wild, natural beauty have long been a magnet for writers, poets and artists. Visited by James Boswell and Dr Samuel Johnson

Left *Located close to the landing stage in Loch na Cuilce, the Loch Coruisk Memorial Hut was built in 1959 in memory of two young climbers who died while climbing Ben Nevis in 1953. The hut can be hired from the Junior Mountaineering Club of Scotland (Glasgow Section). For more information visit: www.glasgowjmcs.org.uk*

during their 18th century journey to the Western Isles and immortalised by Sir Walter Scott in his poem *The Lord of The Isles* following his visit in 1814, the loch has also been painted by many famous artists such as J M W Turner, Sidney Percy and Alexander Lydon.

The tune used for the famous song *The Skye Boat Song* was first heard by Annie MacLeod while being rowed across to Loch Coruisk from Elgol in the 1870s. The music to a Gaelic air being sung by the rowers was written down by Annie and the lyrics were later added by Sir Harold Boulton and jointly published by the pair in 1884.

MYTHS AND LEGENDS

It is hardly surprising that dark and remote Loch Coruisk is said to be haunted by a monster known as an 'uraisg'. Apparently the beast is half-goat and half-human with sharp claws and fangs covered in long and unkempt long hair. An overnight stay around the loch could certainly be a scary experience!

NATURAL HISTORY

A Site of Special Scientific Interest, a Special Protection Area and a Special Area of Conservation, the Cuillins around Loch Coruisk are also designated as a Golden Eagle Special Protection Area. Visitors to the loch may be lucky to see one of the several breeding pairs of this magnificent bird of prey that are supported by this important protection zone.

Most visitors to the loch take the short sea crossing from Elgol (see BOAT

Below *Usually shrouded in mist and low cloud the Black Cuillin peaks around Loch Coruisk are a popular destination for climbers from around the world.*

Hire/How to Get There). Depending on the time of year there are regular sightings from the boats of seals with their pups, basking shark, dolphin, porpoise and minke whale. The boat trips are also a must for bird watchers – recent sightings include sea eagle, manx shearwater, puffin, great northern and black throated diver and eider duck.

WALKING AND CLIMBING

For visitors by boat from Elgol there is but a short clamber over rocks from the jetty to the southern end of Loch Coruisk. Most visitors walk along the southern shore of the loch before returning via the same route. The more adventurous may take a circular route around the boggy shore but the going can be difficult in places. In any event suitable footwear and waterproof clothing is an absolute must in this remote location.

Probably involving an overnight camp, Loch Coruisk can also be reached on foot via a long walk from Sligachan, Kilmarie or Elgol. These are not recommended for the faint-hearted and should only be undertaken by experienced and fit individuals.

The route from Elgol is particularly hazardous involving crossing two rivers and negotiating the infamous 'Bad Step'.

With their 12 Munros, the soaring peaks of the Black Cuillins – the highest is Sgurr Alasdair (3,253ft) – are a magnet to climbers from around the world. Only experienced and fit climbers should attempt to enter the Cuillins and even then it is recommended that they are accompanied by guides. For more information visit: www.skyeguides.co.uk

CANOEING AND KAYAKING

Loch Coruisk and the surrounding Cuillins are a popular destination for sea kayakers and wild campers. For more information visit: www.skyakadventures.com

BOAT HIRE/HOW TO GET THERE

Apart from the choice of several long treks across the mountains, Loch Coruisk can be reached by boat from Elgol. Operating between Easter and October two local boat companies offer trips to Loch Coruisk from this picturesque harbour village which is reached via the long and tortuous B8083 from Broadford. Wildlife trips around the Skye coastline and visits to the Small Isles are also available. For more details contact:

Bella Jane Boat Trips
Tel. +44 (0) 1471 866244
Website: www.bellajane.co.uk

Misty Isle Boat Trips
Tel. +44 (0) 1471 866288
Website: www.mistyisleboattrips.co.uk

TOURIST INFORMATION AND ACCOMMODATION

Broadford Tourist Information Centre, The Car Park, Broadford, Isle of Skye IV49 9AB
Tel. +44 (0) 8452 255121
Website: www.visitscotland.com

Right *The easiest access to Loch Coruisk is via the four-mile boat trip from the village of Elgol. It is but a short distance over rocks from the small jetty in Loch na Cluiche to the southern end of the loch.*

Below *Loch Coruisk can be also reached on foot from Sligachan on the A87 Broadford to Portree road. The 6½-mile path up Glen Sligachan ends on the northern shore of the loch alongside the tumbling outlet from tiny Loch a Choire Riabhaich.*

LOCH MAREE

LOCH MAREE VITAL STATISTICS
Max. length: 12.4mi
Surface area: 11mi²
Average depth: 124ft
Max. depth: 374ft
Water volume: 236 billion gallons

ORDNANCE SURVEY 1: 50,000 LANDRANGER MAP No. 19

Loch Maree is the fourth largest loch in Scotland and contains over 30 islands of which the largest, Eilean Subhainn, is the only island in Britain to contain a loch that, in turn, also contains an island. The islands, now protected as a National Nature Reserve, are home to some of the few remaining remnants of the ancient Caledonian Pine Forest which took root over 8,000 years ago. Overlooking the southeastern end of the loch is the Beinn Eighe National Nature Reserve which, when established in 1951, became the first of its kind in Britain. Beinn Eighe is also of great geological interest - it was formed by massive

movements in the earth's crust over 400 million years ago when Torridonian sandstone was pushed upwards, ending up on top of younger quartzite rocks.

HISTORY

The shores around Loch Maree have been inhabited for thousands of years, their native pinewoods once providing unlimited supplies of wood for building and fuel.

In the 7th century AD, early Christian missionaries from Ireland came to this pagan region. Prominent among them was St Mael Ruba (642-722) who founded a monastery at Applecross in 672. The remains of a chapel, graveyard, holy well and holy tree on an island in Loch Maree are attributed to him - Eilean Maolruibhe is named after him. Sometimes linked with Scottish druids, the island has a darker

side to it – records reveal that bulls were sacrificed here until the 1700s and an oak 'Wish Tree', superstitiously covered with hammered in coins, was even visited by Queen Victoria in 1877.

Located only four miles from the sea at its northwestern extremity, Loch Maree had also attracted Viking settlers by the 10th century. The remains of one of their circular duns can be seen on Eilean Ruairidh Mor, an island which was later used as a place of safety by the Mackenzies of Gairloch, secure from attack by the warring MacLeods. This was no isolated incident of bloody clan warfare around the shores of Loch Maree – in the late 14th century the heads of raiders killed by Black Murdo of Kintail were washed up at Anancaun (Ford of the Heads) at the southeastern end of the loch. This gory find certainly sent out a grim warning to other would-be raiders.

By the early 17th century one of the first ironworks in northern Scotland had been established at Letterewe, halfway along Loch Maree's northern shore. Charcoal produced from locally felled timber fuelled its furnace, the remains of which can be seen today on the lochside.

Above *There are over 30 uninhabited islands on Loch Maree. Home to some of the last remnants of the ancient Caledonian Pine Forest, they are now protected as a National Nature Reserve.*

Below *Viewed from above Tollie Bay at the northwestern extremity of the loch, Loch Maree stretches for some 12 miles through the mountains of Wester Ross.*

Above *In their search for water these gnarled tree roots spread like tentacles over the rocky shoreline of Loch Maree.*

Below *The sheltered bays on Loch Maree's southern shore are overlooked by the mist shrouded peak of Slioch (3,218ft). The highest peak on the north shore, the south ridge of this Munro is reached via an eight-mile track from Kinlochewe to Letterewe.*

Around the early 18th, Loch Maree became known by its current name, commemorating St Mael Ruba who brought Christianity to the region. Until then it had been known as Loch Ewe, hence today's local settlements with names ending in 'ewe'.

Fortunately for the crofters around Loch Maree the worst excesses of the Highland 'Clearances' in the early 19th century passed them by - their good luck attributed to a combination of kindly landlords and well managed crofts.

MYTHS AND LEGENDS
Along with many other Scottish lochs, Loch Maree has its own 'monster' known as the Muc-sheilch. Legend has it that it also inhabits other neighbouring lochs but attempts to find it in the mid-19th century failed. Some say that it is just a very large eel. The waters of the tiny loch on one of the five main islands, Eilean Maolruibh, are said to have magical powers - it is said that being submerged in them can cure lunacy.

NATURAL HISTORY
Containing some of the last remnants of the ancient Caledonian pine forest, the majority of the uninhabited and undisturbed islands of Loch Maree are now a National Nature Reserve managed by Scottish Natural Heritage.

The island of Eilean Ruairidh Mor, planted with pines in the early 19th century, forms part of the Forestry Commission's Slattadale Forest located on the northwestern shore of the loch. The forest is mainly mixed conifers with important pockets of ancient oak and birch woodland. Visitors are well catered for with two car parks and picnic sites - one by the lochside and the other beside Victoria Falls, a local beauty spot.

At the southern end of the loch is Beinn Eighe, its northern slopes the site of Britain's first National Nature Reserve. Also a site of Special Scientific Interest and a Special Area of Conservation, it is mostly owned by Scottish Natural Heritage, with 1,500 acres owned by the National Trust of Scotland. Famed worldwide for its ancient pine forest, wildlife and geology, the 10,000-acre reserve stretches from the loch's shores to the rugged mountain peaks and is home to a wide variety of rare plant, insect and animal species, including dwarf willow and juniper, alpine moss, golden-ringed dragonfly, northern eggar moth, wild cat, pine marten, mountain hare, red squirrel, ptarmigan, crossbill and golden eagle. A visitor centre and car park beside the A832 west of Kinlochewe is the start of several waymarked trails through the reserve.

WALKING AND CLIMBING
From the Beinn Eighe visitor centre there are several trails for walkers up through the pinewoods and out onto the lower slopes of the mountains. Stout footwear is recommended. An eight-mile track also leads from Kinlochewe along the northern shore of the loch to Letterewe. From here there is good access for the ascent of Slioch (3,281ft).

In addition to Slioch to the north, the mountain of Beinn Eighe to the south offers many tantilising peaks for Munro lovers, amoung them Sail Mhor (3,214ft) and Ruadh-stac Mor (3,312ft).

CANOEING AND KAYAKING
There are numerous access points, including three car parks, from the A832 along the southern shore of the loch. A word of caution: Weather conditions can change rapidly and turn the loch into a dangerous place.

ANGLING AND BOAT HIRE
Loch Maree was once renowned for its sea trout but numbers have declined considerably in recent years. For information, permits and boat hire contact Loch Maree Hotel (Tel. +44 (0) 1445 760288) or Kinlochewe Hotel, Kinlochewe (Tel. +44 (0) 1445 760253).

TOURIST INFORMATION AND ACCOMMODATION
Gairloch Tourist Information Centre, Achtercairn, Gairloch IV22 2DN. Tel. +44 (0) 1445 712071.
Website: www.visithighlands.com

LOCH ASSYNT

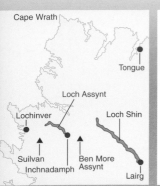

**LOCH ASSYNT
VITAL STATISTICS**
Max. length: 6mi
Surface area: 3.8mi²
Average depth: 131ft
Max. depth: 282ft
Water volume: 86
billion gallons

ORDNANCE
SURVEY 1: 50,000
LANDRANGER MAP
No. 15

Below *Now visited by tourists from all over the world, Ardvreck Castle was once the scene of clan violence, bloodshed and sieges. Changing hands in the 17th century, the castle finally succumbed to an act of God when it was struck by lightning in 1795. In the early 20th century a nine-hole golf course was laid out around the ruins.*

The area around Loch Assynt is a remote wilderness of mountains and heather moorland with a patchwork of lochs and lochans. The mountains are made up mainly from red-brown sandstones belonging to the Torridon Group, which were deposited by enormous river systems around 1,000 million years ago. Beneath the sandstone is Lewisian Gneiss, a rock which was formed around 2,800 million years ago making it the oldest in Britain and one of the oldest on Earth. The landscape we see today was formed by the scouring of the ice sheets and glaciers that once covered Scotland to a depth of several kilometres during the last Ice Age.

Assynt's unique geology draws geologists from around the world and its importance has been recognised by UNESCO who have listed this northwest region of Scotland as Europe's first Geopark. The park takes in around 770mi² of mountain, peatland, beach, forest and coastline across west Sutherland and up to the north coast. The eastern boundary follows the Moine Thrust Zone, an internationally significant geological structure that helped 19th century geologists understand how the world's mountain ranges were formed. Visitors to Assynt can find out more about the Geopark by visiting the Knockan Crag National

Nature Reserve visitor centre which is located on the A835, 13 miles north of Ullapool.

For full details of the Geopark visit: www.northwest-highlands-geopark.org.uk

At the eastern end of Loch Assynt the Inchnadamph National Nature Reserve is a region of limestone caves reached along a dried up river bed along Gleann Dubh. This part of Assynt has a long association with professional geologists who studied the area in the 19th century. Excavations in the caves have revealed animal bones over 11,000 years old.

HISTORY

Excavated in 1925, a chambered cairn set on a knoll overlooking Ardvreck Castle is evidence of human occupation around the loch dating back to around 2,000BC. Farming later became important around the loch and there is much evidence that the land supported cattle grazing, the gowing of corn and even fruit orchards. Excavations have also uncovered traces of a kiln barn, corn mill, dairy and iron workings.

The eastern end of Loch Assynt is dominated today by the ruins of Ardvreck Castle and Calda House. The castle, built in a naturally defensive position on a small promontory, was the 15th century seat of the MacLeods of Assynt. Originally built around 1490 by Angus Mor III, the tower, cellars and vault over the great hall were added during the 16th century. In 1650 the Marquis of Montrose sought shelter in the castle after losing the Battle of Carbisdale to Covenanter forces. However, he was betrayed by the wife of Neil MacLeod and taken to Edinburgh where he was executed. During its short life the castle was the scene of much clan violence and bloodshed culminating in a two-week siege by the Mackenzies of Wester Ross in 1672 after which the Macleods lost their lands in Assynt. The castle was destroyed in a fire after being struck by lightning in 1795.

On the shore close to the castle lie the ruins of Calda House. This was built in 1726 by Kenneth Mackenzie of Assynt for his wife, Frances, who objected to living in the cold and damp of the nearby castle. For its time the design of the house was very modern and was the first of its type to be built in the region. The Mackenzies' stay at the house was short - with mounting debts they were forced to sell it to the Earl of Sutherland in 1736. A year later the house was looted and burned down by supporters

of the Mackenzies and it has remained ruined ever since.

There is a car park conveniently close to Ardvreck Castle and Calda house at the side of the A837.

MYTHS AND LEGENDS

Myths and legends abound about Scottish lochs. Apparently a 'water-horse' similar to those seen on other Scottish lochs, such as Loch Arkaig, has also been spotted swimming in Loch Assynt but details remain sketchy.

The loch is also supposed to be haunted by the weeping daughter of a MacLeod chief, who drowned in the loch after marrying the Devil in a pact to save her father's castle. The ruins of Ardvreck Castle are also said to be haunted by a tall man in grey. Perhaps a visit to the castle on a dark night would confirm a paranormal sighting.

NATURAL HISTORY

With its high peaks and crags, beaches and small rocky bays, the open landscape around Loch Assynt is rich in birdlife. With patience and a good pair of binoculars black and red-throated divers can sometimes be seen on the water, while ringed plover, dunlin, oystercatcher and greenshank can be found nesting on the shore. Pied wagtails even nest in the ruins of the castle while raptors such as kestrel, merlin, buzzards and golden eagle can be seen above the surrounding slopes. Recently sighted again after many years of absence are osprey which once nested in the ruins of the castle tower.

Other wildlife regularly seen around the loch are the loveable water vole and black rabbit - sightings of the pine marten and wild cat are rare but they are known to inhabit the area.

For more details about Assynt's wildlife visit the Assynt Centre in nearby Lochinver or visit: www.assynt.info

WALKING AND CLIMBING

Two good bases from which to explore Assynt's dramatic scenery are both located at Inchnadamph at the eastern end of the loch:

Inchnadamph Hotel
Tel. +44 (0)1571 822202
Website: www.inchnadamphhotel.co.uk

Right *This monument to geologists Ben Peach and John Horne stands on a grassy knoll overlooking Loch Assynt near Inchnadamph. Between 1883 and 1897 Peach and Horne unravelled the geological structure of the Highlands when they discovered the first thrust fault in the world - the Moine Thrust. Since then the area around Loch Assynt has become a mecca for geologists.*

Inchnadamph Lodge Hostel
Tel. +44 (0)1571 822218
Website: www. inch-lodge.co.uk

From Inchnadamph a footpath leads up Gleann Dubh to the Inchnadamph National Nature Reserve and the famous Bone Caves. For the more serious walker a longer path that follows the lower contours of Beinn Uidhe leads to Britain's highest waterfall, Eas a' Chual Aluinn. With a sheer drop of 658ft it is three times higher than Niagara Falls and is a spectacular sight when in full flow.

For Munro lovers the closest peaks, and the highest in Sutherland, are Ben More Assynt and Conival. The rest of the Assynt mountains are just as impressive and include iconic peaks such as Suilven and Stac Pollaidh.

For a shorter and less demanding walk the trail to Loch Leitir Easaidh and Loch na h-Innse Fraoich can be reached from a car park adjacent to the A837 at the west end of the loch. Further west at Little Assynt there is another car park with a footpath leading to the River Inver. When in full spate this outflow from Loch Assynt to the sea is a dramatic sight.

Above *Faced with huge debts the Mackenzies of Assynt sold Calda House to the Earl of Sutherland in 1736. A year later the house was looted and burned down by supporters of the Mackenzies and it has remained ruined ever since.*

Below *Home to wild brown trout and Arctic char and visited by salmon making the journey up the River Inver, Loch Assynt and the numerous other small lochs in this region are a popular destination for anglers. In the distance the twin peaks of Spidean Coinich (left) and Sail Gharbh (right) beckon adventurous hillclimbers.*

For full details of walking in Assynt visit the Assynt Centre in Lochinver or visit: www.assynt.info

CANOEING AND KAYAKING

Access to the loch is from the A837 that runs along the northern shore between Skiag Bridge and Little Assynt. There are three car parks along this stetch of road.

ANGLING AND BOAT HIRE

With its numerous lochs and lochans the Assynt region is also a paradise for anglers. Salmon and native brown trout are found in Loch Assynt along with Arctic char while the large cannibal ferox trout visits shallow pools along the lochside during the night. A large minnow population provides food for fish-eating birds and the Arctic char.

Right *The tumbling waters of the River Inver are visited every year by salmon making their way up to Loch Assynt.*

Much of the area around the loch is managed by the Assynt Angling Group who issue permits and supply hire boats on many local lochs, including Assynt. For more details visit: www.assyntangling.co.uk Fishing permits are also readily available from the Assynt Centre in Lochinver or at local hotels.

TOURIST INFORMATION AND ACCOMMODATION

Assynt Visitor Centre, Main Street, Lochinver, By Lairg, IV27 4LX
Tel. +44(0)1571 844373
Website: www.assynt.info

LOCH SHIN

LOCH SHIN
VITAL STATISTICS
Max. length: 16.7mi
Surface area: 8.7mi²
Average depth: 82ft
Max. depth: 160ft
Water volume: 124
billion gallons

ORDNANCE
SURVEY 1: 50,000
LANDRANGER MAP
No. 16

Loch Shin is the largest loch in Sutherland, a county in northwest Scotland that has some of the most dramatic scenery in Europe. Scoured and moulded by glaciers during the last Ice Age much of Sutherland now falls within the North West Highlands Geopark which contains some of the oldest rocks found on Earth, such as Lewisian Gneiss. The eastern boundary of the Geopark roughly follows the line of the Moine Thrust Zone, an important geological structure. For more information visit: www.northwest-highlands-geopark.org.uk

HISTORY

Located at the southern end of Loch Shin the village of Lairg is one of the few places of any size in this part of sparsely-populated Sutherland. Evidence of human habitation dating back to the Neolithic period can be found on the slopes of Ord Hill south of the village. Here, there are remains of chambered cairns, hut circles and a later field system and settlement. Remains of brochs or defensive towers found at several locations on the southern shores of the loch are evidence of Iron Age settlers in the area.

In more recent times the lands around Loch Shin have witnessed some of the darkest years in Scottish history. By the beginning of the 19th century the 1.5 million-acre Sutherland Estates, owned by the Countess of Sutherland and her husband the Marquess of Stafford, was the largest private estate in Europe. The thousands of people living on the estate were seen as a liability and an obstruction to the introduction of modern farming techniques. In what is now known as the Highland Clearances crofters and their families were forcibly evicted from their homes in Sutherland, many being given a one way ticket to North America. Under the watchful eye of the Countess of Sutherland's factor, Patrick Sellar, crofts were set on fire and, between 1811 and 1821, over 15,000 people were made homeless.

Later attempts to tame the land - around 2,000 acres were ploughed up north of Lairg in the 1870s - were unsuccessful. A monument erected to commemorate this stands three miles north of Lairg near the hamlet of Achfrish. Sheep farming and forestry are now the order of the day around the shores of Loch Shin.

Despite his lack of success with agricultural change the Duke of

Above *Set on a wooded hillside overlooking Loch Shin near Sallachy House is this beautiful grave of Count Ludwig Anton Von Saurma Hoym (1925-2004), a descendant of the House of Habsburg.*

Below *With a length of nearly 17 miles Loch Shin is the largest loch in Sutherland. The waters in the loch rose by more than 30ft on completion of the hydro-electric dam at Lairg in 1960. In the distance is the peak of Meall nan Con, the nearest Munro to the loch.*

Sutherland did succeed in opening up this remote region to railways. With his support the Highland Railway first reached Lairg in 1865 when it opened part of its circuitous route from Dingwall to Wick and Thurso. The Far North line was completed in 1871 and its opening certainly arrested the continuing depopulation of the region. Dependent on large government subsidies, the line is still open today.

As is common with many other Scottish lochs the waters of Loch Shin have been harnessed for hydro-electricity generation. Built during the 1950s the dam at Lairg raised the level of the loch by over 30 feet and created the small loch to the south known as Little Loch Shin. Further to the south are the famous Falls of Shin (now owned by Harrods) with their spectacular salmon leap. A fish lift at the Lairg Dam also allows the migration of salmon.

NATURAL HISTORY

While world famous for its wild brown trout, Loch Shin is also a popular venue for birdwatchers. Raptors such as peregrine falcon, hen harrier, kestrel and

Below *Ruins of Iron Age brochs such as this one north of Sallachy House, can be found at three locations around the southern shoreline of Loch Shin. These drystone, hollow-walled defensive structures can only be found in Scotland.*

buzzard are common sights above the surrounding rolling heather moorland and forests while bullfinch, siskin, wagtail, greenfinch, dunnock, cross-bill, and great, coal, blue and long-tailed tits can be seen around the shoreline. Just off the A836 one mile north of Lairg, a bird hide close to the lochside offers the chance to see black and red-throated divers and cormorants – even the mighty osprey has made a comeback and has been seen fishing in the loch in recent years.

The moorlands and forests to the west of Lairg form part of the Sallachy Estate which is home to a wide range of wildlife including otter, pine marten, wild cat and red deer. For more details about visiting the Sallachy Estate, its facilities including accommodation, shooting and fishing and viewing the Aurora Borealis telephone +44 (0) 1549 402242 or visit: www.sallachyestate.co.uk

Below *Loch Shin is fed by many tributaries and also from the River Cassley via a 2½-mile tunnel to a small power station (seen here on the left) on the northwestern shore of the loch. The total output of the Loch Shin hydro-electric scheme, including power stations at Lairg Dam and Inveran, is 38 megawatts.*

WALKING AND CYCLING

Apart from the village of Lairg at the south end of the loch the only other good base for walkers or cyclists is at Overscaig Hotel on the A838 at the north end of the loch. From Lairg there are good walks to be had along a six-mile-long track that closely follows the western shore from Sallachy House (www.sallachyestate.co.uk)

From Overscaig Hotel (see ANGLING AND BOAT HIRE) there are excellent walks around the north end of the loch. Three miles south of the hotel a track leads from the A838 at Flag Bridge up through wooded Glen Fiag to the ruined lodge on the shore of Loch Fiag.

For cyclists the A838 is a relatively quiet road that closely follows nearly the entire eastern shore of the loch. The nearest mountain bike trail – the Highland Wild Cat Trails at Golspie – is over an hour's drive from Overscaig.

CANOEING AND KAYAKING

Access to the loch is from the A838 that runs down most of the eastern side of the loch or below the Overscaig Hotel. There are several good wild camping sites along the loch and a commercial campsite in Lairg. As usual, midges can be a problem during the summer months.

ANGLING AND BOAT HIRE

Loch Shin is famed worldwide for its wild brown trout. Salmon are rarer but the loch and Loch Merkland to the north have a population of Arctic char that can occasionally be caught on the fly. Fishermen should head for the Overscaig Hotel on the A838 at the north end of the loch. The hotel will arange any necessary permits, provide hire boats and even supply a ghillie for the day. Salmon fishing on nearby rivers can also be arranged. For more details contact the hotel:
Tel. +44(0)1549 431203
Website: www.overscaighotel.co.uk

TOURIST INFORMATION AND ACCOMMODATION

Ferrycroft Tourist Information Centre, Lairg, Sutherland IV27 4TP
Tel. +44(0)1549 402160
Website: www.highland.gov.uk

INDEX

Dubh Lochan, Rowardenan Forest, near Loch Lomond.

Loch Arkaig reflections, The Highlands.

CHAPTER OPENER PHOTOGRAPHS

Pages 10-11
Southwest Scotland
Loch Ken is a long and narrow finger of water set in an area of outstanding natural beauty. Its popularity as a watersports venue appears to sit comfortably with its importance as an environmentally sensitive area.

Pages 24-25
Argyll, The Trossachs and Fife
The natural beauty of Loch Earn has made it a popular destination since Victorian times for tourists, anglers and water sports enthusiasts escaping the hustle and bustle of the big cities.

Pages 62-63
The Highlands
Reached only by train to Corrour Station on the West Highland Line, Loch Ossian nestles between numerous Munros in the 52,000-acre wilderness of the Corrour Estate.

Pages 130-131
Northwest Scotland
With a length of 17 miles, Loch Shin is the largest loch in Sutherland. The waters in the loch rose by more than 30ft on completion of the hydro-electric dam at Lairg in 1960.